ZULMA REYO

EMERGENCE OF CONSCIOUSNESS

DEATH OF THE EGO

First published in 2024 by Zulma Reyo

in partnership with LightEn Publishing

light-en.org
7 Clifford Street London W1S 2FT

ISBN English Print : 978-1-916746-10-7
ISBN English eBook: 978-1-916746-11-4

Cover design by Dominic Forbes

Interior page design and layout by Karen Lilje

All illustrations by Cameron Gray, except where otherwise credited.

Printed and bound by CPI Group (UK) Ltd, Croydon, CR0 4YY

The manufacturer's authorised representative in the EU for product safety is: eucomply OÜ - Pärnu mnt 139b-14, 11317 Tallinn, Estonia, hello@ eucompliancepartner.com, www.eucompliancepartner.com

LIGHT EN
LIBRARY OF LIGHT

To my beloved students, whose courage to face life and themselves in the pursuit of Truth never ceases to amaze and inspire me.

TESTIMONIALS
*Written by students who undertook the death and rebirth process
at the Zulma Reyo School of Consciousness*

I undertook the death and rebirth process outlined in this book over a two-week period at the Zulma Reyo School of Consciousness. It was both the most painful and the most beautiful experience of my life. This process enabled me to truly take responsibility for absolutely everything in my life — EVERYTHING. At the end of it, I felt a love of self and for all of creation beyond any that I had yet experienced. I had a deep understanding that my Presence was my inspiration and my True Love. I saw how I had caused pain and experienced great pain throughout my fifty years of life, but I 'departed' with the deep knowing that I had not failed and neither had those whose paths had connected with mine, no matter how great the trauma. This was more than Forgiveness. This was Freedom and this was Love.

KH (Cohort I)

The process of death and rebirth is the most challenging, transformative, and liberating spiritual and personal journey I have ever undergone. I have been able to confront my deepest shadows, face them head-on, and acknowledge that they reside within me. I have also remembered that I have been a victim of abuse, manipulation, and abandonment that occurred when I was a child, leaving imprints on my beliefs and personality that hindered my ability to expand my potential. I have sought help from psychologists and therapy sessions and have been a part of some of the most renowned spiritual foundations in the world, such as the Art of Living. All of them have helped me, but nothing compares to the depth of this process. This comes from within, from facing oneself. I was accustomed to clearly discerning when external factors harmed me, and I didn't want to or couldn't acknowledge that the power lay within me, that it depended on me. It was uncomfortable, and personally, I preferred to avoid it. It was easier and more understandable to blame my parents, my circumstances, even my fear. Realising that I have caused harm and have been harmed, forgiving others, forgiving myself from the heart, has allowed me to live my daily life as a new man, a better husband, a better father, a better entrepreneur, and above all, a BETTER I AM.

MP (Cohort 3)

The death and rebirth experience was profoundly life-changing for me because it allowed me to leave behind low-frequency energies that I had held all my life but had belonged to my mother's traumas. I now understand they were hers and not my responsibility to carry! Shedding them was a viscerally liberating experience and has set me free to be me and feel who I really AM! This has brought so much balance, light, love, and joy back to my life to enjoy and give back to the World! I am forever grateful!

CS (COHORT 2)

Zulma's profound work on death and rebirth has touched the very core of my being. As I experienced the transformative journey, I found myself facing the depths of my own soul, confronting the darkest corners of my existence. It was a process marked by the poignant release of my past burdens and a magnificent reawakening. Through this life-altering odyssey, I came to embrace a profound understanding — that authentic forgiveness starts with the act of forgiving oneself. As I let go of the burdens I had carried for so long, I unearthed a newfound peace that radiated from within. This experience transcended that of a mere rebirth; it was a metamorphosis of the soul. I realised that the true essence of life lies not in accumulating possessions or achievements but in the chance to focus on personal growth and the relentless pursuit of becoming a superior version of oneself. Zulma's teachings have brilliantly illuminated my path, serving as a perpetual reminder that in forgiveness, letting go, and finding inner peace, we unlock the door to our own transformation, and therein lies the key to a life truly well-lived.

LC (COHORT 4)

Dying is living. And to live is to learn to Love. To love myself, to love you, to love one another. Having the deep desire to vibrate from this state of Being is only compatible with strongly embracing life, leaving behind the extra burden of the emotional and mental dimensions that limit me and make it difficult to advance in my life purpose. The deeper I went into the core experiences of my life, the more obvious it became to see how everything makes sense within a greater plan. This realisation has helped me enormously to have a wiser, more luminous, and compassionate view of myself and others. With total freedom, acceptance, and responsibility to be what I am. I have the total conviction that going through the process of death and rebirth is an internal call from the soul to undress myself before the mirror of my life, to dare to look beyond who appears reflected and find myself in front of what I truly am. I feel that this purification process is indispensable for everyone who is on the path of service to humanity. This is what led me to look for Zulma and be part of the School of Consciousness. With gratitude to share these precious moments together.

ZV (COHORT 3)

Guided by my teacher, Zulma, and her expert team, I embarked on a profound journey of death and rebirth. Their consistent presence offered me a deep well of support as I ventured into the depths of my personal history, my pain, and my very soul. With unwavering courage, I opened my heart, allowing the release, forgiveness, and healing processes to unfold, ultimately enabling me to bid farewell to what I once believed defined me. I came to realise that it was merely my life's narrative, not my true essence. It served as a toolbox, allowing me to uncover the 'WHAT FOR?' of my experiences rather than fixating on the 'WHY?'. During meditation, I transcended individuality and became one with the sun, earth, air, and the cosmos. My vibration harmonised with the stars, resulting in a blissful rebirth that intimately connected me with the sheer joy of life.

SL (Cohort 4)

I was fortunate enough to experience the death and rebirth process as part of the Inner Alchemy course offered by the Zulma Reyo School of Consciousness. I felt a little apprehensive before the process because the word death can evoke fear, and I was unclear about what or who would die. The death and rebirth process became the most valuable, life-changing experience I have had, because it enabled me to truly see how my patterns and personality traits have run the show thus far. I was carefully guided through breaking the layers of my personality to access my Presence, my Self. I was able to release and process many emotions that had been suppressed. By doing so, I could see how my expectations had hurt others, how my pain and abandonment had played out. I felt love like I had never felt love before and was able to feel compassion, forgiveness, and love for those around me, especially those who had caused me the most pain. I felt the gift of freedom. From this experience, I made new life contracts, which I have since lived by. As a result, my life has changed, and my relationships have changed all for the better. The process allowed me to identify the many patterns I had repeated and gave me an opportunity to let go of them. What dies is the parts of the personality that no longer serve you, the ego. And what is born is a new version of you, with all the love, truth, and wisdom gained from this experience.

VJ (Cohort I)

Undertaking the process of death and rebirth at the Zulma Reyo School of Consciousness was about experiencing both pain and joy, confronting both the angels and the demons within me, and aligning both mind and emotions in order to find the intuition of the heart. For me, the process of death and rebirth marked a course of transformation that not only uprooted a lot of pain but also led to a path of cleansing and healing. This experience is a powerful tool for understanding that we can, with clarity, discover our true SELF and allow it to express itself through words and actions.

TF (Cohort 3)

No one ever wants to be confronted by their own mortality. We go through life with some kind of collective attention deficit disorder, anaesthetised to the deeper questions life asks of us. But how would you feel if you knew that you had only two weeks left to live on this earth? That's exactly the experience I faced during the death and rebirth module at the Zulma Reyo School of Consciousness. Fascinating and frightening in equal measure. It forced me to confront who I had been for over 50 years and how different that was from the person I thought I was. Yet in finding forgiveness for my own mistakes, I was able to forgive others through the painful memories and the life lessons they offered. In having my own eyes opened to the inner beauty of all people — friends, family, and even foes — I was able to find the beauty in myself.

GB (Cohort 2)

For me, the process of death and rebirth implied a radical change in the perspective of my life, what I had created, and what I really am. It meant taking responsibility for my creations, my life, and my relationships, and not blaming anyone, including myself, for it. Seeing all this through the eyes of my Divine Presence and embracing it from there, myself and all the people who are part of my life (family, friends, enemies…). It meant hitting rock bottom, feeling the deep pain that we carry inside and from which we escape all our lives. To no longer escape and face it, to feel that pain and to be able to hold it with love, filling that enormous void within with the light of my I AM. And, in this entire process, you humanise yourself, and you realise that your pain is the pain of humanity. This makes you have a new, more compassionate and loving perspective on yourself and the rest of your brothers and sisters. The great gift that this whole process bequeathed to me is having the certainty that I am not alone, that my I AM sustains me, and that death does not exist. Not only knowing this, but having lived it and experienced it in myself, which is precisely what happens in this process, gives you a radically different perspective on life. It puts you in a situation of absolute inner power, in complete trust in yourself and in God, who always supports you. This changes your inner world and, with it, the outer one so that fear dissipates, and you can give and be an example of love, able to take this great Truth to the rest of the people around you. The result is to live at peace with yourself and the world, understanding human pain in a more compassionate way, while living life in light and in fullness. It is knowing how to see with the eyes of the heart.

EL (Cohort 3)

PERSONAL THANKS

My debt to the people who enable and care for me is infinite. In this spirit, my dedicated team of teachers and students at the Zulma Reyo School of Consciousness heads the long list of thank-yous for discovering each day, and every moment, that life is precious and eternal. The latest, but not least, of the beautiful people who grace my life is Colm Holland, my much-more-than-editor, soul-brother friend, who appeared in my life like an angel of light and clear vision, putting my rather long-winded, somewhat poetic prose into perspective and coherence. I must express my gratitude to him and to Valerie, who embraces and inspires him the same way he does me with my writing.

Zulma Reyo

CONTENTS

LIST OF ILLUSTRATIONS AND DIAGRAMS

GLOSSARY OF KEY TERMS

Alchemical Alignment

An energy circuit formed by linking the Earth and the heavens. It shifts perception from the ordinary, denser awareness of lower physical, emotional, and mental energies to the elevated perspective of the Spirit-Self. Its practice affects the body's physical cellular structure by recalibrating it in patterns of Light-substance. It is also known as the Alchemical Circuit and the Master Practice.

Angels, Guides, Spirit Friends

These are entities dwelling in higher dimensional planes, who surround and assist embodied humans to realise their original goals for a current embodiment.

A human being is assigned a Guardian Angel, but he or she also incorporates the influence of other angels that work under the great teachers and masters of higher dimensional life. All angels respond instantly to the call of humans, as their mission is to emanate the qualities or virtues they embody. Their main objective is to infuse a person's aura with the particular quality deemed most needed, whether that be peace, courage, or love.

Guides may comprise any number of human beings no longer inhabiting the physical plane, who have vowed to help humanity. Every human being has guides. Their work is tireless and most often unacknowledged by humans. A guide may also work within the tutorship and greater aura of a Master. Every human being, conscious or not, is also under the guidance of a Master to whom their soul ray belongs.

Spirit Friends exert a positive influence on an individual's super-consciousness, attracted by either a former direct relation or a kindred resonance with an embodied human being.

Astral and Astral Realm

The astral realm is a multifaceted phenomenon. The lower astral dimension mirrors the third dimension and is an energy field of vibrationally lower thoughtforms that magnify self-centred, unconscious behaviour. The upper astral realm reflects benign, higher-frequency thoughtforms. The astral realm includes astral entities, 'shells' of human beings bound to physical existence.

Aura, Auric Field

The energy field surrounding a human body that reflects the nature and the quality of the energy fields or bodies generating it. (See *Etheric Body* overleaf).

Bardo

In the Tibetan tradition, the *Bardo*, or *Bardo Thodol* as it is sometimes called, is an intermediate, transitional, or liminal state between physical death and rebirth.

Being, States of Being, Dimensions of Being

'Being', or 'Being state', refers to the primary, formless experience of Spirit as manifest Consciousness. This is one step down vibrationally from unmanifest Spirit. Being is very close to soul and is a generic name for individualised Spirit. Being expresses itself dimensionally as various 'states' of Being.

Consciousness and consciousness

When written as Consciousness, it is the first and primary expression of Spirit and Source. When written as consciousness, it denotes the activity of awareness in an embodied human being.

Dimensions

The dimensions are stages of adaptation of the Spirit-Self that become progressively denser as it journeys into physical embodiment. Each stage defines a capacity of Intelligence to handle elements that range from vast cosmic consciousness to the minutest detail in matter.

Ego, Ego-Self

The ego is the Self's necessary and unique personal perspective within incarnation. The personality is built around its ego structure. Ego is the casement (which is differentiated in each lifetime) for the expression of soul. It is the energetic entity that houses the essential individuality, the ultimate personal 'I' that serves as a tool for the greater Spirit-Self, I AM. This is the meaning behind 'I am that I AM', an affirmation to be repeated continuously.

Egoism and Ego-Death

Ego must be distinguished from egoism, which is the self-centred personality, and clearing the ego of egoism is referred to as ego-death. It is a process whereby embodied individuality is purified of its lower astral attachments. The purpose of our work is to retain the uniqueness of the personal Self while dissolving the impurities that clutter it, such as the basic fears of survival, the preoccupation with self-importance, and the need for dominance.

Electronic Solar Presence

This is the name given to the Presence of the individual God-Self, or that aspect of the Spirit-Self that pertains to the Absolute Infinite State of Beingness, which some refer to as God. It is sensed as an intense electronic field of frequencies beyond the human range that, in its fullness, resembles a radiant sun. It is also called the Sun Presence, or the I AM Presence, resonating within the heart of each embodied human as the personal I AM.

Etheric Body, Etheric Double, Etheric Counterpart

The Etheric Body is an exact replica of the physical body, but where the physical body is made of matter, the etheric is composed of subtle substance, made up of lines of force that manifest themselves inside the physical body as energy pathways.

The Great Work

Also known as the Master Practice, the Great Work is the traditional alchemical term used to invoke the *Alchemical Alignment*.

Self, Higher Self, Higher Intelligence, Higher Spirit, Higher Mind, Christ Self, Intelligence-Presence

The Higher Self, as distinguished from the lower self, is elevated human awareness in a higher frequency 'body'. When the personality has integrated its lower bodies of experience in matter, it aligns with its state of Being as soul, becoming a fully conscious personality. The Higher Self, or Intelligence-Presence, is a frequency of holistic or Higher Intelligence, which then allows the personality to function interdimensionally. The human evolutionary purpose is to reach and sustain this vibrationally higher form of self and become soul-infused.

Indwelling force

The indwelling force within a human being is invariably soul influence, which always seeks expression, regardless of the individual's level of awareness. For us, it represents the force for good.

Karma, Karmic Board

The Sanskrit term for the feedback circle of energy created by an individual through their interaction with others and with life. It is commonly referred to as the 'law of cause and effect'. There is a 'positive' and a 'negative' karma. The Karmic Board, also known as the Lords of Karma, is an energy body of eight ascended masters who are assigned the responsibility to dispense justice and to adjudicate karma, mercy, and judgement on behalf of each soul on Earth.

Light, Light Nucleus, Home

When written as Light, it is the emission of Spirit or Source: the core of matter and its transmuting agent. Your Home is Light.

When written as light, it denotes the usual definition of it as electromagnetic radiation. Light and light function similarly to reveal the essence of reality.

Oneness, Law of One, Law of Light, Law of Love

Oneness, or the Law of One, refers to the non-existence of separation or duality. When the mind takes on the all-embracing qualities of Light, thinking is raised beyond the polar perspective of matter to the level of Higher Mind, which operates in accordance with the Law of One. The individual then perceives the world differently: they begin to understand the workings of the whole. Mind and emotions take on a new expression, becoming more refined and compassionate.

Personal Energy Bodies (PEBs)

The Personal Energy Bodies (PEBs) are entire energy fields, or 'bodies', to do with physical, emotional, or mental activity. They relate to the lower-dimensional needs of the personality and have little to do with Spirit-Self.

Personal Focus of Consciousness (PFC)

The Personal Focus of Consciousness (PFC) designates a mobile and subjective centre of attention that encompasses our personal priorities. The PFC may be directed either by the unconscious or automatic personality or by the conscious personality (the Higher Self).

Psyche

The Psyche is understood as the nature of the personal self that encompasses its emotional desire nature. This ranges from the vast astral realms between the lowest instinctual aberrations to the most affectionate ownership deployed in personal attachments and relationships. It is also the personal identity as seen through relationships with others.

Psychic Nature

The 'psychic nature' of a person is an aspect of their emotional receptivity. Psychic nature equates roughly to 'the emotional desire nature' covering the vast astral realms between the lowest instinctual aberrations and the most affectionate ownership deployed in personal attachments and relationships. Anything that refers to the personality self, its needs and wants, falls within the category of 'psychic or emotional nature'. Dimensionally, the psychic realm corresponds to the shadow of the third dimension: that which may or may not have materialised into concrete things or experiences. This enables a person to tune into other people's thoughts and feelings as if they were real or their own.

Reincarnation, Rebirth, Renaissance

These terms denote the stage of re-incorporation of a Spirit-Self into the physical plane known as the third dimension. Each term means the same thing, although each also sheds light onto a slightly different aspect of re-embodiment. Reincarnation: into the flesh. Rebirth: into a new cycle. Renaissance: born anew.

Service

Service relates to the many forms taken as the true purpose of the Spirit-Self's embodiment in the world. It includes the selfless focus of energy and action towards humanity and service of the Light.

Soul

A state of Being vibrationally midway between Spirit and body, soul is a vehicle for Spirit and harbours the stock experiences and integrated lessons achieved through many incarnational cycles. Both container and content, the soul is the intermediary between the lower self (manifested human being) and Spirit.

Source, Spirit, Truth, Essence, the Absolute

The unmanifest principle of Oneness, Essence, the Absolute and Truth behind all Creation.

Spark

The Spark defines an atomic-like particle of essence that is emitted from the Absolute or Spirit as a replica of itself. It is cast on a journey that courses through various densities of Light-substance and dimensional life before embedding itself into matter and acquiring the DNA coating of parental lineage. It is the nucleus of embodied human Consciousness as Light within matter.

Third-Dimensional Personality

The personality can only be a three-dimensional entity. When used together with the word 'three-dimensional', it stresses the fact that it is an ordinary personality, not yet refined into the confines of the higher, more illumined mind.

Void Clear Light

This is the vision one might have of Everythingness, or the All; too bright to distinguish any form and apparently empty of all form. This is also the stage of maximum enlightenment possible in Tibetan Buddhist terminology during the *Bardo* stage when Consciousness folds back into its Self. It describes the superconscious experience of the newly departed after the separation of spirit from its body casement; only possible when and if the deceased has attained a state of desirelessness or enlightenment capable of merging with the highest frequencies of cosmic essence. It is clear because it contains everything. It is void because it is empty of all earthly meaning.

Wheel of Fortune

An eight-rayed wheel that illustrates the motion, the sequential and eternal cycles of the natural world and is connected to the Wheel of Karma.

AUTHOR'S PREFACE

It often seems to me as if I am constantly dying and being reborn. Sometimes I cannot relate to the person I was last year, or even last month — and yet something of who I was then, as if it were fifty years or lifetimes ago, filters through and connects all the people I have been.

Zulma Reyo, *Inner Alchemy*

When I wrote the revised edition of *Inner Alchemy,* I included a brief mention of my thoughts on, and experiences with, death and dying.[1]

My intention was always to expand on those thoughts because they deserve much greater treatment than was possible at the time. That is why this book was born. My thinking has gone through many layers of death and rebirth, long before the words reached these pages. One of the important lessons of life is that every aspect of becoming embodies elements of death, and the process of true spiritual work always requires that we die and be reborn.

I explained in *Inner Alchemy* that our embodiment lends Consciousness the texture of matter as clothing, which, subject to the laws of nature, decays and eventually disintegrates. Physical death is like changing clothing: unveiling and living the transparency of Spirit-Self as the indwelling Consciousness.

The truth is that you are constantly dying. Every outbreath is a spontaneous release of energies, residues of thought and feeling; every in-breath offers a new possibility for expression, bringing in new air (or Light). You are dying every day. Every night you go to sleep, you are dying and then are reborn when you awake. Every major energetic experience you have is a sort of death; even the act of love itself is a death experience. Such is our physical life.

How you experience and respond to death emotionally and mentally while still in embodiment is intrinsic to spiritual development. You must apply yourself to the transformation of the egoism, fostering modalities that are in tune with the emerging soul. *Inner Alchemy* deliberately

> The truth is that you are constantly dying. Every outbreath is a spontaneous release of energies, residues of thought and feeling.

---

1 **Reyo, Z.** (2021). *Inner Alchemy: The Path of Mastery.* LightEn Publishing. pp. 279–281.

provokes disidentification with both body and personality from the beginning while cultivating authenticity and individuation at the level of consciousness. This is done by transferring the point of reference from a separate self to a broad spiritual awareness. By following the process of *Inner Alchemy,* you can give birth to yourself or, in other words, remould your energy bodies in accordance with the original patterns of perfection dictated by Spirit, transforming or restructuring the personality.

There is infinity beyond physical life. The journey through the afterlife, as revealed through ancient teaching down the ages, exposes you to more strenuous trials than those presented in daily life. Each spiritual path will require that you learn discernment, surrender, appropriate resistance, and an ability to sustain heightened levels of intensity and focus. You are asked to develop the ability to resist illusion and those thoughtforms that make up your emotional and mental baggage. You are shown how to embody power in its various expressions. You are encouraged to silence the chatter of the mind in order to perceive the real behind the illusory, and you are taught how to still the whirlpools of emotions by developing purpose and integrity.

To succeed in your journey through the afterlife is to attain levels of mastery; to fail is to be thrust into a lower level of life to which your habits have attracted you.

Death provides you with the opportunity for supreme alchemy.

But you do not need to wait for the moment of physical death to initiate this transformation. The process begins with you, now.

I have been writing and lecturing on the subject of death for well over four decades and it is still challenging. People are as attracted to this subject as they are resistant to it and fearful of it. In order to speak about death and dying, we must confront life, and few are willing to embrace the totality of their lives: the good with the not-so-good.

A person is rarely content with the course of their life, regretting many decisions, nostalgic over some moments and with many unlived impulses still waiting to be fulfilled. Nobody wants to leap into unknown territory loaded with fantasies that mirror the superstitious mood of their lives, and there never seems to have been enough time to carry out their desires. Yet most haunting of all is the glaring fact that few understand the meaning of life. To live the totality of one's life and view it all with

> Each spiritual path will require that you learn discernment, surrender, appropriate resistance, and an ability to sustain heightened levels of intensity and focus.

serenity, maturity, and gratitude is the task of those who have embraced the essence of time and timelessness.

We speak about embracing the eternal present, God, or Consciousness. The mysterious depth of NOW is inexplicably fascinating, untouchable, and challenging. It cannot be understood through rational means. It is the essence of silence, meditation, prayer, and communion, along with that ineluctable texture life takes on when it meets the boundaries of death and discovers the continuity of spirit life.

The short, simple, and in many ways terrifying truth for those who prefer a concrete, conditioned, and uncomplicated existence is that we are eternal, formless Beings. When we die, we cease to be as we know ourselves. Death marks the end of personality with its manageable boundaries and limitations. Only the notion we hold of ourselves in connection with the laws of matter dies, i.e. those confines that make life controllable.

The body functions as the home for personal identity. Death implies growing into the totality of ourselves beyond appearances. Everything we cling to (in the belief that concrete, definable things and the people we hold dear bring us joy) is transitory — shifting elements on the stage of becoming.

Rather than 'being' as an experience of each moment and stage of our life, we focus on 'doing'. Rather than live reality, we perpetually substitute it with illusions. Meanwhile, the flow of life offers delights and pleasures beyond imagining — immaterial experiences that cushion and decorate the scaffolding of our conceptions.

Your real job is to bridge the heavens and the Earth within you, reconciling the Presence with the personality and opening the physical body to enable the embodiment of the soul: this is the real Rebirth.

Many of us are incapable of digesting the emptiness of fullness, the essence of 'now' that are contained in life as in death. Instead, we demand concrete answers to the experience of the 'now', and mistakenly fill our lives with so many expectations and theories about death and what lies beyond it. If we wish to know what death is about, all we need to do is delve deeply into the way we live every moment of each day.

Rather than being what you *do,* death displays what you *are*. What is this insistence on controlling life that the mass of humanity pursues? It reveals another reason why death is taboo: because so many of us perceive

Rather than being what you do, death displays what you are.

life as a logical continuity where the aggressive force of personal will conquers all obstacles. In a logical world, dying is wholly illogical, but in a spontaneous, amazing whirlwind of perpetual stimulating (holistic) motion, life is endless. The first perspective relies on the ordinary activity of the mind as linear and sequential; the second defines a state of understanding that is intuitive yet chaotic, thrilling and pulsing with infinite life. The latter way of thinking also functions at another deeper level as the mind of the meditator: the secret spice of the inner world and inner reality.

I am not the first person to say that to know about dying, you must be willing to allow every moment of your past to die. But how do you die when you have not fully lived? Life, if lived fully, prepares us for death. The quality of one reveals the quality of the other. If you lead an unconscious, accidental, superficial life or a painful one filled with challenges and defeat, death will merely be a cessation — a long-awaited peaceful ending to all those soured or uneventful years. (Then again, it might be the privation of what you considered a successful life.)

If, on the other hand, you have led a full life, enjoying both depth and width, as well as ups and downs, death will seem like a natural closure, an end to a stage of becoming. It will be a challenge you will meet one hundred percent, just as you met and overcame so many other seemingly incomprehensible challenges in life. Every experience leads to another new and unexpected one, unprecedented and unrepeatable. Dying is just one more: a sort of metamorphosis into a beautiful ephemeral butterfly.

I dreamed I was a butterfly, flitting around in the sky; then I awoke.
Now I wonder: Am I a man who dreamt of being a butterfly,
or am I a butterfly dreaming that I am a man?

CHUANG TZU

My friend, as you read this book, I welcome you to Life.

Zulma Reyo
Mallorca 2023

—

Life, if lived fully, prepares us for death. The quality of one reveals the quality of the other.

—

ACKNOWLEDGEMENT OF SOURCES

While writing this work, I referred to various books, essays, and other sources over so many years that it is impossible to name them all. The major direct sources on death and dying are obvious: *The Tibetan Book of The Dead, The Egyptian Book of The Dead*, and *The Popol Vuh (Mexican/ Mayan Book of The Dead)*.

The information on the details of dying, and most especially embodying, is drawn from personal recall in meditative states as I traced my own lives back through time. Some of the information I gathered personally has been verified in spiritual classics, but much has not been confirmed by outer sources beyond my own inner circle of my mother, aunts, and uncles, all based on information they obtained through mediumistic means.

I myself partook in a spiritual rescue circle for some years in Kent, U.K., working in collaboration with spiritual guides 'from the other side' to help confused disembodied humans by orienting them towards places of learning where they could obtain information on what had happened to them and learn what to do. It was the most significant work I did to research this important subject, and I then set out my findings in this book.

My life and work have been particularly influenced by an amazing series of books written in Spanish but, as yet, untranslated: *Orígenes de la Civilización Adámica* by Hilarión de Monte Nebo (Josefa de Luque Alvarez), as well as *Phillip in the Spheres* by Alice Gilbert, and *The Red Lion: Elixir of Eternal Life* by Maria Szepes (which traces a series of embodiments of one person) also had a tremendous influence on my teaching and understanding of life.

No book of spiritual significance could stand without the wealth bequeathed by the early teachers of the Theosophical Society.[2] I have benefitted from studying most of them.

---

2 For further reference, please see the Library of Light and resources at www.light-en.org.

INTRODUCTION

To teach people to live without fear is to teach people to live. And dying is the biggest fear.

WHY DO WE FEAR DEATH?

When we think about death, most of us are immediately struck with fear and anguish. After all, physical death can occur at any moment, and we have very little control over it. This nearly universal fear of death derives from the false belief that we *are* what we *think*.

To understand this, you only need to look at how predominant the use of rational thinking is in the ways most of us identify and understand ourselves. Our identity is wholly dependent upon who and what we believe ourselves to be, and our rather illusory conclusions that define us. We relate to one another accordingly and feel a need to continually evaluate our relationships and the conditions of our lives, regularly searching for meaning in our circumstances and obsessing over our artificially conceived daily schedules.

This nearly universal fear of death derives from the false belief that we are what we think.

In truth, most of our lives are enslaved to the ways we think about and associate with things, and to the memories we carry with us. Even the most private, inner moments of our subjective lives are ruled by our logic-cutting, linear thought processes. Sensitivity and spontaneity, not to speak of our reactions to the unexpected, are usually at a bare minimum.

None of this is helpful when we enter our authentic inner world. It is wholly separate from the identities we give ourselves (including the memories that give these false identities meaning and the feelings that give them emotional power).

FINDING OUR IDENTITY

Our true identity is that hidden part of ourselves that is more real than any of those external, artificial facets of our lives.

Through a finely honed feeling-sensing faculty, one that remains largely undeveloped in most of us, we can perceive the voice of our soul and its yearnings. It is a voice that quells our greatest fear, which is death and the lack of apparent continuity it brings.

In our upbringing, especially in modern Western cultures, no real education is provided to help us understand our soulfulness or explain our innermost yearnings — what they represent and why they are there. This only intensifies our feelings of fear towards anything that is not solid, provable, and permanent.

For many, death is an experience of anticipated loss and separation, threatening to rip us from our habitual patterns and the relationships we cherish. Many instinctively sense that, while dying, a person can continue to see and feel but cannot do, touch, or experience anything other than through the emotions and associations that prevailed in their life. Without the physical shell that acts as a buffer to the impulses, reflexes, and myriad energetic phenomena that interact with life on all levels, emotions are actually stronger during the first stage of departure.

Yet the emotional awareness of the physical world that has given meaning to the newly departed lasts only as long as their attention is held on friends, places, and conditions. In the transition between life and death, this degree of attention corresponds to one's level of attachment, personal focus, and interest in affairs and people at the third-dimensional physical plane.

In other words, the mind attaches to the objects and people it must leave behind, especially to those who cry out to them. Only those who have rid themselves of possessiveness and personal needs while they are still alive, including the vices that replace love and meaning, will be released from this fate. And those who listen attentively will hear the still small voice within, which speaks of another mysterious reality.

On the following pages, you will find a remedy to our ill-informed understanding surrounding death — one that will illuminate the reality of our sustained connection to Spirit. It will expose this communion and its relationship to our real purpose in embodiment and will lay bare the power of your Spirit. As a result, you will gain an understanding of Creation and creativity.

GIVING BIRTH TO YOURSELF

The crucial training of giving birth to yourself begins once you shift your attention away from the immediate physical needs of your third-dimensional personality and focus instead on the aspirations and the indwelling force of Consciousness: that elusive Spirit-soul within.

Once you grasp this essential Truth, you can create a tangible link, a camaraderie, a companionship with the forces of Light at the highest level — and you can do so while you are still embodied. Rather than a comfortable, pleasurable life filled with self-indulgence (which you sometimes fool yourself into believing is still altruistic), your greater purpose is to fulfil a higher life-calling, which emerges at the level of Spirit beyond embodiment.

A human being is so much more than their personal life. Each of our journeys contributes to the creation of a better humanity and a better world. Life is eternal, but not in any way you can envision from the physical perspective. Eternity is more magnificent than you can even imagine.

This book is more than just information; it is meant to guide you through revelations that will annihilate the egoism aspect of your ego. Through conscious dying or release within this embodiment, you can be reborn even during your ordinary lifetime.

Once you grasp this essential Truth, you can create a tangible link, a camaraderie, a companionship with the forces of Light at the highest level — and you can do so while you are still embodied.

As with all *Inner Alchemy* material, the principles expressed in the primary book,[1] especially the Master Practice of *Alchemical Alignment* repeated below,[2] must be observed and applied. That's because they provide the link between our human existence and our cosmic identity in a multidimensional journey between existence and essence: the transition from the 'I' who is here now to the 'I AM' in eternity.

THE JOURNEY THROUGH THE AFTERLIFE

It is important for the living to let go of their departing loved ones and try to generate a feeling of celebration and gratitude, remembering the quaint, funny, endearing moments but not clinging to their own needs or perpetuating the relationship. Most people will struggle with this idea because it collapses the entire edifice upon which they build their lives. Unless they are educated in the perception of transcendent life and its purpose, the ones who remain behind will face a sense of meaninglessness and must learn to cope, if they can, without the crutch of their beloved. It is extremely difficult to understand the interpenetrating, interweaving dynamics of life and death while attached to the utility and meaning that a special someone might represent.

The initial period of the departed's keen awareness of and connection with the world they have left behind is short-lived. After a review of their life, the deceased is pulled away by their own greater spiritual force. Some of those left behind may, through meditation, have been able to accompany a loved one during this transition, yet this too is partial and temporary. The physically embodied cannot participate in the private, intimate communion between Spirit and the dissolving identity because the conditions of embodiment prohibit this.

Eventually, the departed must journey alone beyond the lower astral planes of emotional content linked to the third dimension by answering a higher call of self-evaluation and transcendence from their Spirit-Self positioned in another dimension. This ultimate experience is one of total transparency in Consciousness: a period of reckoning and confrontation with their personality self and the world they have shaped. This is a

---

1   See *Inner Alchemy*, pp. 21–22, for further discussion of these principles.
2   See *Inner Alchemy*, pp. 142–147.

period of accountability to the divine within. Every action and role they have taken in life, and the use made of the earthly substance of the physical body and the world, along with the faculties associated with this use, comes under review.

This all-encompassing task can only happen alone. This stage, beyond personal recollections and feeling, is the part that frightens the living when they think about death: the discontinuity, the helplessness, the exposure, the lack of foresight and control, and the issues lodged in our personal attachments and interests.

However, the reality of Higher Mind[3] and our real nature as Spirit Consciousness will inevitably remain unknown and ignored by those without proper curiosity, sensibility, and training. Yet this reality is always present, either in the voice of the soul or in dreams, through angelic intervention or as spirit guidance.

By following the principles and processes I have outlined in this book, you will not only benefit your own journey through death and rebirth but also help advance the well-being of society and the positive changes in the world that are desperately needed now more than ever.

This begins with each one of us. Our work consists of clearing ourselves of borrowed opinions and ego attachments that pollute the mind with insistently selfish thoughts, self-aggrandising emotions, and gnawing instincts. When you cling to your notion of separation, you contribute to the astral pollution of collective humanity through your every thought, word, and deed. You also assure yourself of a long and painful *Bardo* (journey) in the afterlife.

The apparently inoffensive habits and secret thoughts harboured by an ordinary person are the stuff of daily life, but they are also nourishment for the lower astral realms that every one of us traverses immediately after separation from the body in death. If, however, you work to clear yourself of these traits while still embodied, refining the personality of egoism and constructing a healthy transparent structure that can attract and house the soul, you assure yourself of a tranquil transition at the moment of death.

The journey through the shadowy, dark realms upon death becomes a clear, smooth, swift path towards the Light; there is nothing to frighten

The apparently inoffensive habits and secret thoughts harboured by an ordinary person are the stuff of daily life, but they are also nourishment for the lower astral realms that every one of us traverses immediately after separation from the body in death.

---

3 See *Inner Alchemy*, pp. 128–9, for further clarification of Higher Mind.

or intimidate you, and there is no compelling desire that you must battle against. The gross instinct and passions have been conquered. This is a good enough reason for us to refine our sensibilities and live with the integrity demanded by the inner Self that calls for peace, joy, and transcendence.

When you prepare for death, with the dying of your egoism, you discover freedom, heaven, and bliss while living a sacred relationship with Spirit.

In the course of dying, as in life, the enemy is fear. Fear forecasts doom and failure. It demands dependence upon others and outer things to 'rescue' or 'save' you and give you a meaning you cannot find within yourself. Fear is the exact opposite of love: they both contain the same voltage, but inversed. While fear retains, love releases. Only the same kind of resistance can neutralise a charge; that's why only love can neutralise fear.

Once you understand this, you will discover a life of freedom and authenticity as you learn that you are not helplessly stuck in a violent world of despairing projections, aggressions, and unpredictable events that seem to control you. You will know that you can restructure your world when you restructure yourself and live ethically, creatively, and according to the laws of Nature and the heavens. But to pierce through that powerful collective miasma of fear, you must learn to see and trust yourself — that is, your true Self.

If you are reading these lines, you are already listening to your 'Self'. Know that when you touch upon the heart of Self, you fall into the spaciousness of the All, where you are never alone.

In the course of dying, as in life, the enemy is fear. Fear forecasts doom and failure.

THE MASTER PRACTICE AND EXPERIENCING THE TEACHINGS IN THIS BOOK

This book is intended to help you go beyond a theoretical understanding of the death and rebirth process. You might find that it satisfies your inquisitiveness on the topic, but until you move beyond the intellect towards an engagement with the Higher Mind, it will remain no more than an interesting read, with few other benefits.

I have specifically structured the content to help you go deeper and further in your pursuit of Consciousness. To assist in this, I have included a selection of meditations I regularly use and teach in my school.[4]

The first of these meditations is the Master Practice — a procedure that aligns the body with the Earth and with cosmic forces. Although it appears in my book *Inner Alchemy* (pp. 22–23), I have included it again here because it is the foundational meditation (and meditating will assist you in an experiential understanding of the material presented in the remainder of this book). I recommend that you pause your reading at this point and begin to practice it and then continue to practice it daily.

By way of a brief introduction to the Master Practice, you should know that the human structure is composed of both Earth-matter and Light. To function as an integrated personality with higher Consciousness, it is essential to acknowledge and understand our human makeup. In meditative states, our body composition leans towards a greater proportion of Light. You can read more about this practice in the chapter *What Is Alchemy? And Why Inner?* (*Inner Alchemy*, page 17).

Inner Alchemy works through visualised and/or sensed energy, using colour, breath, and sometimes sound to create Light forms that act through the body, environment, or situation evoked.

Take a look at the four steps of the meditation in the illustration overleaf. They take you through what I call the *Alchemical Alignment*, which is the purpose of the Master Practice. This also enables you to engage with the Electronic Solar Presence, which is the name given to the Presence of the individual God-Self.

Inner Alchemy works through visualised and/or sensed energy, using colour, breath, and sometimes sound to create Light forms that act through the body, environment, or situation evoked.

---

4 Zulma Reyo School of Consciousness: www.zrsoc.com.

The Alchemical Alignment

Step one of the Alchemical Alignment

Step two of the Alchemical Alignment

Step three of the Alchemical Alignment

Step four of the Alchemical Alignment

STEP ONE

Spirit emanates a current or ray of Light directly into the head of a human being. This current represents the lifestream. It flows down the spinal column to the base, spreading into the nervous system. This induces sentient life in matter.

STEP TWO

Notice that the human figure is mirrored by an inverse figure of Light below. This represents the grounding of the Self, where this wholly luminous and transparent figure of Light is connected to Earth's centre.

STEP THREE

Nourishment is now received from two sources: from the Cosmos (Consciousness) and the Earth (and the vitality of frequency, her Light). In this way, the body is, in reality, a passageway between the heavens and the Earth.

STEP FOUR

The student then uses visualisation to invoke the Tube of Light, as seen in the illustration. This tube enfolds the body, including the mirrored Light body. It acts as protection, enabling the student to remain centred within the frequency of Light while engaged in everyday life. From this perspective, the human self is acknowledged and embraced.

Take care to perform the following Master Practice meditation slowly, and with intent. One way you could do this, and the other practices suggested throughout the book, is to record them in your own voice and set the meditation to music. The Master Practice may take as long or as little time as you like; a daily practice of at least 20 minutes is recommended.

THE ALCHEMICAL ALIGNMENT

Light-life follows attention.

Sense the body. This is very different from your regular consciousness when thoughts and emotions are allowed to wander freely.

Scan through different areas, activating visualisation of the body parts together with in-depth sensation. This is how frequencies are modulated, affecting health and physical well-being.

Feel every part of the body. Breathe consciously until the body feels balanced and whole. Breathe with a stress on body stability, density, and weight, producing a sense of solidity and safety.

Now direct your attention to the Earth below.

Evoke a subtle electric current from the figure of Light mirroring your physical form, absorbing its vitality on the in-breath and pulling the sensation upwards slowly through the body. This Light triggers an awakening at the centre of each atom, which responds in kind. Concentrate on each part of the illumination process.

On the outbreath, eject all excess thought, emotion, and density through the feet into the figure of Light that absorbs this.

Feel how electricity and expansiveness suffuse the whole body, giving it a sense of physical lightness and extension into the surrounding space. Imagine and sense the powerful presence of Light above the head. Direct your full attention upwards to the Sun Presence, visualised above. The higher you direct your attention, the greater frequencies of Light are reached. Sense this.

Focus on the feeling, as if you are in the middle of an ocean of Light without beginning or end. All is limitless space.

Rest. Allow the experience of fullness and impress this quality into your memory so you can evoke it at will.

From that sublimated stance, which is identified with Spirit, direct attention down to the physical self. Compassion flows inwardly into the lower (physical) self. Acknowledge the flow of energy into your cells. Feel how much you are loved by Spirit.

Before returning, visualise and sense the Tube of Light descending over and around you, including the figure of Light, protecting and enabling high frequencies in the body.

Very gently and gradually come back to the initial stage in the body and modulate your frequency inversely towards greater weight and density. Know that you have the capacity to tune into other vibrations and states of being, and that no intermediaries are needed.

The path towards genuine independence and liberation has begun. Statements such as 'we perceive what (where) we place our attention on' (in other words where our interests are) and 'we create our own reality' now begin to make sense.

Know that you have the capacity to tune into other vibrations and states of being, and that no intermediaries are needed.

PART ONE

EMBODIMENT

Before delving further into an understanding of the disembodiment of the Spirit-Self from the physical body, it will be helpful to remind you of your origins. It is worth noting that each time you embody, you do so under the guidance and protection of your Spirit-Self. Furthermore, every life has a mission of Service, whether you recognise it or not.

The Master Practice

INITIAL DESCENT

During our initial descent, Consciousness first travels through the upper vibratory range of Spirit frequencies, basking in the light of itself, enamoured of its proximity to Source and its own creative powers. As the journey continues, it dips ever steadily into denser and denser vibrations

The Spark

as it approaches the material planes. Each step downward results in an ever-greater definition as it distances itself from the original Oneness. This is a happy journey filled with the seeds of hope and renewal. Consciousness dresses itself with dimensional Light-substance and eventually approaches the heavier elements of matter that culminate in the third dimension.

During the first part of the journey, the frequency decelerates gradually in response to the new, self-created environment and the confines of increasingly limiting and qualifying conditions. Higher Intelligence adapts itself to the corresponding mental and sensory faculties induced at each state of Being at each dimension of its descent. Then Consciousness gives life to the various dimensions of itself, each emitting distinct qualities as States of Being. This process is repeated at each rung of the dimensional ladder and can later be perceived by us as various worlds or 'realities'.

Here is a short summary of the qualities that the Dimensional levels of Consciousness give life to in the descent from Original Spirit to Embodiment.

THE DESCENT FROM ORIGINAL SPIRIT TO EMBODIMENT

Original Spirit

Twelfth Dimension: fusion, total quietude, plenitude, emptiness

Eleventh Dimension: ardent aspiration, devotion, unconditional dedication

Tenth Dimension: contemplation, silence, peace

Ninth Dimension: state of knowing, seeing

Eighth Dimension: focused intention, searching – the 'eureka' dimension

Seventh Dimension: integration, intuition

Sixth Dimension: discernment, creativity

Fifth Dimension: planning, probabilities

Fourth Dimension: reflection, restructuring

Third Dimension: senses and concrete mind

Second and First Dimensions: rhythm and pulsation

Embodiment

At the journey's midway point (halfway between original Spirit and the third dimension), the vibratory field pulses equally with the frequencies of Higher Spirit and Lower Earth life. The energetic experience of yourself as the Spark at this stage is similar to a pearl dropping into a semi-dense flow of liquid, multicoloured Light-substance.

This experience is recalled during our physical embodiment through our subliminal Light memory, which accounts for our innermost experience of inspiration. This midway point also marks the last outpost of divine influence before the rules and restrictions of Natural Law kick in, as material density and weight take effect. This is also the stage where the embodying Spirit collects any remnants of unfinished business from former incarnations in order to complete old lessons in a new setting. It is here that it contacts the soul, which is the repository of former integrated experience.

THE PULL OF EARTH

The second level of the journey begins the moment Consciousness approaches Earth's gravitational pull. Spirit attracts matter in the process of condensing and adapting itself to the Laws of Nature into which it is incorporating. In this act, the returning Spirit consolidates its twofold nature as both Light and Matter. This is the moment when Consciousness begins to weave a physical form with the help of Nature Spirits, absorbing the nutrients from our biological mother during the process of knitting together the material bodies. Time is now sensed by the embodying Spirit as separate, with distinct lapses, and our form and structure are bound by its standards. You are also limited to a very particular location in space. Even so, Consciousness, the original core of our Being, forever remains linked to Light and its calling, although in a state that is somewhat dulled and muffled from this point onwards during its embodiment in matter.

Consciousness, the original core of our Being, forever remains linked to Light and its calling.

The Pull of the Earth

MATERIALISATION

The next stage is materialisation. Our physical and psychological makeup develops as a result of our Spirit's intention, which is now faintly laced into the imprints received from our biological parents. The Light-form of our material existence is also determined by our chosen life purpose or Service. This plan unites with the traits acquired from our parents to shape our individual being. The result is a distinct body-heart-consciousness pattern that shapes not only the physical body but also our emotional nature.

The Integration of Consciousness

In short, the Light-seed or Spark enters Earth's atmosphere dressed in a coat of many colours; these colours are arranged in a unique, predetermined way to support its primary purpose or Service in embodying. The whole process is supervised by the Spirit-Self from a higher dimensional perspective, who will, on occasion, voluntarily step into the womb experience. Finally, the emerging entity integrates with the planet's whole history, as it absorbs unfinished lessons from previous incarnations, and the new incarnation reflects past personal tendencies and attachments.

The experience of the developing foetus follows an adhesion to progressively more complex material structures that the Light of Consciousness infuses with life. At the early stage, the foetus is also accompanied by a host of Spirit Friends from the upper planes. As it gradually absorbs the surrounding energy field, the newly forming infant body also slowly absorbs the emotional context of its new family. At the last stage, Consciousness is covered with a heavier, denser liquid Light that allows for the full mental integration of the Light-form to its earthly environment.

As this deceleration process continues, more of the surrounding influences are absorbed into the substance of the child. Matter and nourishment are drawn from the mother's psyche and experiences, as are the genetic memories from the ancestral line and the collective environment. Now, the original Spark, nestled within a tiny, undeveloped body, gives birth to the heart, which is the first construction that the Spark's life force creates in matter.

Once the fully formed foetus is born into the third-dimensional world, the new incarnation is equipped with the basic tools needed for its life plan of Service.

The exact time and place of birth are chosen with this plan in mind. What began as a Spark of pure diamond Light slowly acquires the form of a star, which then becomes a sphere around the Light-seed, coalescing into the mould of a human shape before finally taking on flesh.

——

What began as a Spark of pure diamond Light slowly acquires the form of a star, which then becomes a sphere around the Light-seed, coalescing into the mould of a human shape before finally taking on flesh.

——

The Shape Forming Process

GUIDES, SPIRIT FRIENDS, AND INFLUENCES

The embodied Being has a live memory imprint of the original archangelic-human. It also brings with it various Guides and Spirit friends who may be perceived by clairvoyants and appear as formations of Light in the aura of the individual. These are star-like and provide access points for nourishment and communication with Source at different dimensional levels.

Initially, the newborn has no memory of higher dimensional life. Instead, its environmental and cultural surroundings provide the bulk of psycho-physical influences. The nature of the Light-form varies during the building of the material form, in part because the entry into the physical plane involves opening to a network of interconnecting lines of forces. These forces appear as grooves or energetic formations on the aura. The pressure of the collapse of substance further anaesthetises the Spirit in preparation for resonance with denser material sensations. The original bright Light-nucleus withdraws into the Heart and Crown Chakras.[5]

During gestation, Spirit influence flows directly through the umbilical cord of the mother feeding the developing foetus not only with earth nutrients but also with the Light force of Spirit in preparation for intelligent autonomous life. Embodied human beings bear two deposits of (cosmic) Spirit energy that are a direct outflow from Source. The two deposits become embedded in the physical body of the newborn at birth. The first portion of Spirit energy-substance (invisible to modern scientific equipment but visible to clairvoyance) is deposited at the base of the spine — a place known as the *Kanda* in ancient Sanskrit. Unless misused through excesses, it supplies each human being with life force throughout their entire existence on Earth. The second portion buries itself in the centre of the brain, barely perceptible during the first months of life. This is the tender area over the crown between the brain's two lobes, which closes soon afterwards. Highly subtle filaments may be sensed here, at this early time, by a clairvoyant.

—

Initially, the newborn has no memory of higher dimensional life. Instead, its environmental and cultural surroundings provide the bulk of psycho-physical influences.

—

5 See pp. 69–86 of *Inner Alchemy* for further information on the Chakras.

The two pockets of Light energy continually emit basic frequencies that feed both the body and the developing intelligence, but their full and higher use remains inaccessible until the individual awakens to their dual nature. At that moment, when the individual gains in Consciousness and is able, through personal effort, to withdraw their fascination with personal desires, they acquire the appropriate level of energy management and tolerance of intensities of Light required by the soul. Now the proportion of Light (Consciousness) within the matter of the body (physical substance) increases, provoking the full activation of Spirit power in embodiment.

Formation of the Heart and Crown Chakras

This is sensed as an energy 'rising', a 'transfiguration', or 'enlightenment' in different ways. When this happens as a direct result of conscientious clearing work of the self, rather than forced through aggressive willpower, it declares to the person's soul, guides, teachers, and masters that they are finally ready to handle cosmic energies with integrity. The person then truly enters the spiritual path.

When Spirit originally descends into matter, it does so through what is referred to as the Current of Light. This passageway of Source lies sealed within the central part of the spinal column, feeding life and Consciousness to the individual. It is also known as the *Sushumna*.

When Consciousness rises to embrace the Spirit-Self nature, the *Kanda*, as life energy, rises through the *Sushumna* as the 'kundalini fire'. Its sheer power awakens the Light sealed in the centre of the head (the Third Eye) by impacting the pituitary and pineal glands jointly, imposing an implosive merger of Light within. At this point, the individual is able to accept and employ the tremendous power and faculty of Spirit while embodied. The original birth connection is regained, only now in matter, and in the fulfilment of its initial plan to bring Spirit into matter and to instil a spiritual life of Service.

This is the same process that is reenacted in death. The appearance of the 'Void Clear Light' marks the encounter of the individual with their original Spirit-Self as the Divine Presence — ego returning Home. Our view is: why wait until physical death to reach this mythical paradise, when you can get there now by doing the 'dirty work' right here on Earth?

—

Why wait until physical death to reach this mythical paradise, when you can get there now by doing the 'dirty work' right here on Earth?

—

PHYSICAL BIRTH AND OTHER TRAUMAS

Birth represents the first trauma for the incoming Spirit, similar to a massive earthquake. Breaking free from the protective haven that harboured it for nine months, the infant takes its first breaths. As the lungs fill with air, Spirit ignites within the new physical structure, accompanied by the shock of foreign sensory exposure. It is the first experience of pain.

A second, simultaneous shock occurs as the new life is ripped from the mother's aura. Now the individual must experience the separation and aloneness of losing the solid connection of the umbilical cord to the

protective physical shelter of the mother's body. This is a sensation that endures throughout their life.

A third shock comes with the invasion of environmental emotions and thoughts from the collective world to which the individual is now exposed, overwhelming the baby's previously placid state.

In some spiritual traditions, birth is considered a far more painful experience than death. The tremendous sense of loss it creates does not heal in our subsequent physical life. Instead, it manifests in the latent instinctual desires towards ever greater sensations and emotions and a need for a clearer definition of and control over life. This was well understood by several ancient cultures, in which painstaking efforts were taken to shelter, embrace, and care for newborn infants. For example, only parents were allowed initial access to the child in order to provide protection through kindred or familial impressions. This was sometimes limited to dwellings of total darkness with no outside contact and could last up to a year before the infant was finally allowed to come into contact with Earth's ground (soil) and other people.

Little by little, the infant defines its separate physical form and adapts to its environment. Progressively, the imprints from the planet attach themselves to the child's auric field, affecting the sensory mechanisms of the body, mind, and emotions. As the embodied Spirit grows older, it collects emotional and mental patterns and thoughtforms.

—

In some spiritual traditions, birth is considered a far more painful experience than death.

—

SELF-DEVELOPMENT

Not even the most inspired and enlightened person can escape a life of separation and confusion marked by the experience of conflict and tension in matter. This is the Natural Law of Polarity. Only when the external forces of self-discipline and purpose as Service are employed as an internal posture can the individual find relief from this condition. Even so, an embodied Consciousness can never be free or fully able to recall its original state of Oneness unless it engages in the spiritual path of self-development.

The Birth Trauma

In addition, engagement with the resonance of being human is essential in order to heal the isolated Spirit from the trauma of separation and set the Personal Focus of Consciousness (PFC) within the heart. Masters, teachers, spiritual friends, and positive influences can provide some nourishment. However, in certain cases, the critical humane touch never comes or occurs too late in life.

FURTHER STAGES OF DEVELOPMENT

With new challenges come new lessons. For instance, at puberty, the personality coalesces around the emerging complexity of the mind and emotions. The physical mould inherited from parents and family usually predominates until adolescence, but with the advent of puberty, another dramatic breakdown occurs that is comparable to birth trauma. Chemical changes cast the growing human out of their comfortable, mundane patterns and set them at odds with their familiar environment.

The process of ego-formation and expression leads to the building of a particular identity as a means to orient and differentiate oneself from the rest of society. Every experience makes an impression, which, in turn, determines how the person responds to and thinks about situations. Defence mechanisms, such as fear and anger, arise as forms of self-protection and preservation, creating energy knots in the body and aura that further reinforce personally conditioned ego behaviour.

The individual's character develops by following the path of least resistance. For Spirit development to occur, arbitrary defence mechanisms must be dissolved through spiritual methods and self-awareness, otherwise, they reappear later in the death process as roadblocks. These obstacle courses stem from fearful emotions — even comforts and loving attachments can become artificial coping mechanisms in life. All memories, as congealed thoughtforms, must eventually be released, because only by letting go of their momentum can their energies reunite with Spirit and return home.

> All memories, as congealed thoughtforms, must eventually be released, because only by letting go of their momentum can their energies reunite with Spirit and return home.

DIMENSIONS OF BEING

As an embodied Spirit, you act at both the lower and the upper dimensions of Being simultaneously, with varying degrees of self-awareness. For instance, the degree of Consciousness you develop manifests around the physical body. At the outermost, subtler layers, the aura's colouration usually appears less pronounced. By contrast, at lower levels, intense personal tones dramatically colour the aura around the physical body and personality. This personality aura displays the working dynamics of the three lower bodies (physical, emotional, and mental) and showcases how the mind, body, and emotions have been used or misused. It can take a lifetime of work to dissolve these personal creations and regain the original transcendent faculties and powers of our Light heritage. Then, it can take even longer to integrate redeemed energies into a personality that can reflect the spiritual qualities of its upper-dimensional coatings. Overleaf are visual representations of the process of dissolving personal creations at the lower auric levels.

Thankfully, embodiment provides ample opportunities to learn how to manage one's personal energies. Relationships, for example, can be especially helpful. Also, quality, enlightened self-help circles, and professional, spiritually-minded therapists may provide support at various stages of life. Individuals who seek to escape from dense thought formations and illusory beliefs often benefit from contemplative prayer and certain forms of meditation. Each of these methods, properly used, can teach how to manage energies in a way that leads to a higher dimensional life. They may even become an avenue to final liberation, whether through the death of the ego in life or the death of the body.

Liberation is not easy, but no life in the body is.

Reconstructing and upgrading our life in physical matter involves integration of our conscious personality with Spirit. This is where the embracing of body, mind, and emotions flows into a cohesive unit and manifests as one's soul purpose.

Once the recognition of being Spirit within a physical body takes place, past conditioning is loosened. The energies encapsulated in matter can then be released and are free to return to the original Source.

Auric Cleaning Sequence

Dark, distorted aura, clogged with thoughtforms

Adhered thoughtforms, including attachments and influences

Cleansed aura

Illustrations created by Patricia Bedin. For further illustrations and descriptions of the auric fields based on perception please see *The Rainbow Bridge* by Two Disciples (available to read at www.light-en.org).

At this point, one reformulates, redeems, and transmutes thoughtforms as personal creations, triggering a remarkable, explosive change.

The alchemical, or transformative, effect of heightened awareness and the release of the Light-force within redeemed matter ignites the buried Spark in each cell linked to the Heart Chakra. This results in an illumination that is sensed in every particle and layer of the body. In this way, a stable link between the soul and Spirit is built.

Then the journey Home into Oneness and Essence truly begins, blazing a trail for all to follow.

There is only one exception to this potential transmutation. It happens when a 'personality shell'[6] (the congealed thoughtform from the personality of a previous incarnation) fails to complete its journey of requalification. In these cases, fear and anger cause the shell to resist the purifying winds of karma (that would otherwise motivate it to reflect upon the consequences of every action taken in life). These winds normally allow for the resolution and ultimate integration of all life's actions.

When the shell resists, it flees and seeks shelter in more 'comfortable' conditions that are inevitably similar to the former limited state, such as the comfortable and familiar surroundings within the shadowy astral realm. This can happen in the death process, just as in life.

An incarnation is originally chosen by the Spirit-Self to advance its spiritual development while helping other incarnate Beings do the same. Occasionally, a soul chooses a difficult life in order to correct former inclinations, learn new lessons, or reach the less fortunate. Sometimes this choice is wholly altruistic and has nothing to do with past personal lives.

The alchemical, or transformative, effect of heightened awareness and the release of the Light-force within redeemed matter ignites the buried Spark in each cell linked to the Heart Chakra.

6   For a detailed explanation of the nature and activity of a 'personality shell' see *Inner Alchemy* pp. 204–206.

PART TWO

DISEMBODIMENT

Developing an identity (also known as an ego or personality) is a lifelong process. It starts with how our awareness adapts to third-dimensional reality, including our physical bodies with their potential for mind and feeling. This development is also influenced by how we handle, or sometimes mishandle, our relationships and experiences as we grow and evolve.

Initially, Spirit Consciousness is barely relevant to the development of an identity and takes a backseat to sensory instinct. Consequently, most people are wholly unprepared for the afterlife and its demands on focus, awareness, integrity, and the ability to stand alone and whole when facing the consequences of their actions. Unless awareness is honed in life, additional training is urgently called for through careful instructions and guidance concerning death and its consequences.

THE RETURN JOURNEY

Upon death, you travel back along the same path you took when embodying, though this time, of course, in the opposite direction. The return journey calls for a reintegration of the faculties of Spirit in the higher dimensions, which you relinquished upon descent. These faculties are not directly required in physical life or for the ethical review called for upon death. This unfamiliarity is the prime reason why the first stages of death can be progressively more difficult. Having lived in ignorance of one's true nature in this embodiment, an encounter with accusing alien voices and memories stored within the inner-Self may be shocking and confusing. This can be followed by fear, anger, and ultimately, denial: a train of emotions that creates havoc for a person who has yet to give up their material identity.

The experience of breaking away from the body's physical matter is an inverse recall of the pressure produced during the trauma of birth. The sudden release into silence can also be disconcerting and may even cause the mind to freeze.

Aspects of the personality are slowly dissolved in the process of dissociation from the identity formed in life. The end result, at this stage, resembles a return to the State of Intelligence that existed before the imprinting by social and planetary influences. At this point, many individuals will flee in fear to what they consider more comfortable and familiar surroundings within the shadowy astral realm — invariably, these will be similar to or worse than those they left on Earth.

Souls who are more practised in managing their mind and emotions may allow themselves to see, feel, and understand how the unravelling of Consciousness relates to their own past use of will. These souls may decide to dwell in happier conditions and might even seek to reorganise themselves and somehow confront the impulses contained within life forces.

DYING WITH PURPOSE

Only a few who have nothing to hide consciously choose to face the Light humbly and unashamedly. In so doing, they affirm the place of Consciousness and release themselves from Karmic pressure and the bonds of matter. Free to serve humanity actively, they do so either by re-embodying with a particular purpose or by participating in the activities of higher-dimensional life. Some may even serve embodied humanity through spiritual influence from the subtle planes. This is the state where the spiritual laws of brotherhood and collaboration prevail. The vehicle is transformed into a vessel for the healing and building of a better world.

Yet, for the average person, death is faced without knowledge of the workings of Consciousness and involves meagre contact with the upper dimensions. Such individuals find their meaning and purpose purely in the material world. They have, at best, only the slightest glimmer of compassion or subconscious memory of their origin in Light. Sometimes, these individuals possess a religious faith in 'God', though it is a 'God' they keep distant and separate from themselves. By contrast, people who are connected to their soul, and have embraced spiritual forces within themselves, can experience divinity as a deeply intimate phenomenon of wholeness.

CONSCIOUS DYING

You may not be aware that you are going through the death process as part of your natural life. Yet you can awaken to its occurrence and, in so doing, participate in the Great Work of Consciousness. To attempt life and death without an active role in the process is to live a life of lesser meaning and purpose. For this reason, you must face up to your fear of death and embrace it wholeheartedly. The following are some guidelines to assist you in dying consciously.

Only a few who have nothing to hide consciously choose to face the Light humbly and unashamedly.

PHYSICAL DEATH AND EGO-DEATH

Dying physically and the death of the egoism of the ego-Self are essentially the same experience. The only difference is in the physical symptoms. When you die, your Spirit-Self sheds your physical shell. When you experience the death of egoism, you shed the illusion of, and attachments to, separation and exclusivity. The latter is a lengthier replica of what occurs during physical death, and you can start preparing yourself for it even while living. As mentioned in the introduction, death may make you fearful because you are afraid of the loss of your identity. This is equally true with ego-death, and this fear is all the more acute when you have not come to terms with your Spirit-Self essence.

Your Spirit-Self is who you truly are.

The memories you carry in your physical cells and the experiences you have accumulated in your psyche are your own creations representing unconscious reactions to physical forces. In this life, you have created who you are through the nature of your responses and how they dictate the ensuing consequences. You are solely responsible for the nature of your existence. Whether it is joyous or full of pain, whether you are asleep or awake, it's all down to you.

This is a concept you might find hard to accept, asking yourself, 'Why do I create such horrible conditions for myself?' One positive answer is this: you must experience life so that you can serve humanity with compassion. The work of *Alchemical Alignment* develops a three-dimensional human resilience and flexibility that enables us to understand and see world dynamics as they unfold.

The Buddha said that suffering is the consequence of desire; therefore, you should eliminate desire and live in a state of desirelessness. You can achieve this once you have faced your deepest human nature with all its components, including your perceived strengths, weaknesses, instincts, and habits. Some apply the Buddha's teaching about suffering at a mental level only. They say, 'I will meditate and close down the desires that clamour for my attention by simply shutting them off'. This only partially helps. The mind must also be prepared to embrace the emotions of the child-self, which is the dominant, archetypal bearer of human nature. With this outline in place, let's dive deeper into each distinct stage of death.

— In this life, you have created who you are through the nature of your responses and how they dictate the ensuing consequences. You are solely responsible for the nature of your existence. —

Consciousness separates from the physical body

Consciousness separates from the personal identity

THE DEATH OF THE BODY

Physical death is where Consciousness — or the Spirit elements of the self — separate from the physical body. This is also where the comparison, or analogy, between physical and ego-death ends. Our physical body disintegrates. Why? Because the Spirit-Self withdraws. Our spiritual self is what animates and gives us life and energy (which some call 'the soul'). When it leaves the body, matter decomposes: ashes to ashes, dust to dust, and earth to earth.

In physical death, the Spirit elements of our self rise to where they came from. This is not a hopeful perspective for those who die with fear of the loss of identity or those who seek escape from their physical life. The greater life of the Spirit-Self forces a resolution: the confrontation with the essential truth that when you die, everything is known.

THE DEATH OF THE EGO

In the process of ego-death, or transformation, truth is revealed little by little. However, in physical death, you cannot escape the impressions you have forged. All those hidden parts of your being that you tried to keep secret from others are fully and immediately exposed. The illusion of lying to yourself is only possible because you are in the material body; once you shed this Earthly form, all the good, the bad, the beautiful, and the ugly stand revealed.

This exposure does not happen (as some people imagine) because there is a divine judge waiting to pronounce a verdict. Instead, the truth is revealed because *you* are the judge — and you cannot lie to yourself. Physical death is not eternal sleep: it is an awakening from which you cannot hide.

Much of the information about these processes is taken from the *Tibetan Book of the Dead*, the *Mexican Book of the Dead*, and the *Egyptian Book of the Dead*. All these ancient teachings share common threads and truths about life after physical death, though I have drawn most heavily from the Tibetan tradition, which I found similar to experiences I had when tracing the process of self-evaluation and reorientation in the afterlife.

Each person interprets and decodes symbols from the subtle world according to their own capacity and tradition, but I find that the sequence of events always follows the same order. Thoughtforms and feeling images pertaining to Earth consciousness return to dust, while the voice of the soul increases and the attraction towards Spirit leads the way into greater Light. This is why I find the terminology of the Tibetan vein, such as Void Clear Light, lapses of time, and the reference to coloured lights and sounds, more fitting than those of other traditions.

—

Physical death is not eternal sleep: it is an awakening from which you cannot hide.

—

The Separation of the Elements of the Physical Body

THE SEPARATION OF THE ELEMENTS OF THE PHYSICAL BODY

In the Tibetan tradition, there are four elements of the physical body that separate at the point of physical death: earth, water, fire, and air.

EARTH MELTING INTO WATER

This is the sensation of merging with the earth, which means pressure, weight, and density. It is the feeling of the body matter melting like lead: pouring and alternating with a sensation of weight. It can be compared to the experience of fainting, where you involuntarily fall to the ground. At this stage, you are still experiencing physical sensations, though you are no longer bound by physical force.

WATER MELTING INTO FIRE

Now the sensation is of intense cold accompanied by perspiration. Energy runs through the body, causing chills and alternating with heat that seems to flood the body like a scorching fever. It can also be compared to the experience of recovering from a strong dose of anaesthetics.

FIRE MELTING INTO AIR

This feels as though the body is inflated with air or gas to the point of becoming unbearable, as if it were about to explode. The sensation is one of bursting or disintegrating into atoms in a complete and explosive dispersion. This feels as though it was generated in the centre of the navel.

AIR DISSOLVING INTO DIAPHANOUS LIGHT

The Etheric Body mould lets go as you experience the other-dimensional forms. For Buddhists, the light at the end of the path is the Void Clear Light. It is void of matter, but it is also everything and so attractive that you want to go there. Unless a close one asks you to stay, or your own desire keeps you on Earth, you will flow into that light and won't come back. The pressure that was building up in the third stage now explodes into Diaphanous Light. Complete silence arises.

For Buddhists, the light at the end of the path is the Void Clear Light. It is void of matter, but it is also everything and so attractive that you want to go there.

THE TRAJECTORY OF CONSCIOUSNESS

Following its release from the physical body, the etheric body now follows a trajectory with four distinct experiences. We refer to these as: (1) first and second consciousness, (2) the reality of the mind (the *Bardo*), (3) the Renaissance, and (4) Reincarnation.

THE DEATH PROCESS AND DIMENSIONAL LEVELS

The First and Second levels of Consciousness are not only about integrating with your experiences but also about taking responsibility for your actions. This will occur on many different levels once you've taken the first major step: facing your life. The illustration below summarises the relationship between the Death Process and the Dimensional Levels.

In the first wave of the death process, you adjust to the intensity produced by the generation of love. You live it; you face it. The next realisation is that everything is within, and it is all ultimately a reflection of you: in the sense of all One-ness, divine unity, and the collective Oneness that you are.

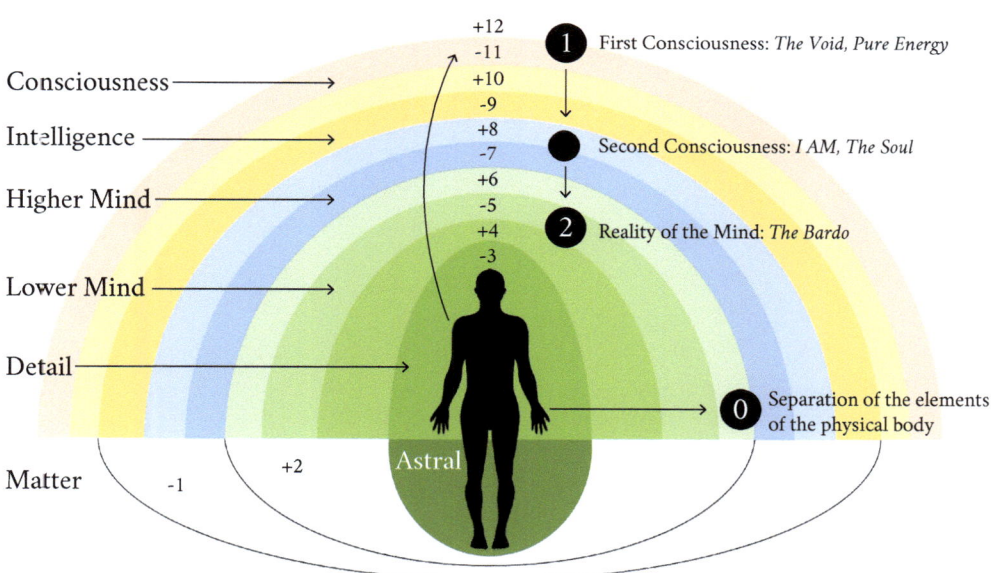

The Death Process and Dimensional Levels
©Lilia Rodrigues

The second wave of the process concerns acceptance without movement: the management of impulse and mobility. This is the longest part, where you fuse with the divine aspects of Consciousness. This takes time because the ego-Self persists for a good while, tempting and seducing you into fixed patterns and instincts until the very end, when you leave it all behind.

At the start of this process,
everything is alive and throbbing with energy.

As you leave your body and begin the journey home, your Consciousness will perceive lights, symbols, and sounds — but without the shell of the physical body for protection. This is particularly difficult to understand while in embodiment because, here on Earth, your human physical form serves as a buffer — a shell securing you from reality at all levels of Consciousness. This, in turn, fosters the illusion of separation.

Some of us are more sensitive to sound, colour, or light. When you leave the physical body, and even in your explorations of dimensional reality in this life, you will find yourself much more sensitive without the physical casement. And later, in the *Bardo*, the emerging sounds may seem to assault your senses, the lights may blind you with their intensity, and you might instinctively resist the unexpected, uninvited phenomena around you by wanting to retreat to your former safe, well-designed physical enclosure. But you cannot. For this reason, in many ancient traditions, preparing for death[7] involves facing and tolerating great frequencies of Light and resonance.

——
When you leave the physical body, and even in your explorations of dimensional reality in this life, you will find yourself much more sensitive without the physical casement.
——

---

7 For a brief outline of Ancient Traditions, see the Appendix in Part Six (p. 141).

FACING THE LIGHT AND EGO-DEATH

Facing the Light — for your soul and Spirit — means facing the pain, facing the depth, facing the loss, facing the fear, facing the violence, facing the anger and any other unresolved resonance from previous incarnations.
This is encountered as ego-death.

A description of the process of ego-death implemented in our School of Consciousness is outlined shortly in 'Part Three: Clearing the Pathway to Becoming' so that you may experience the truth of these teachings and learn how to 'die to live'.

When you face the Light energies, or forces of life, you do not feel 'attacked', even though Light, like love, is intense. The hardest thing for you to accept as a human being is that you are loved, not for what you do but for your essential nature, for what you are!

It is scarier to feel complete love than to feel hatred.

Because love can be more devastating to the ego than hatred.

Love kills the ego. Love takes you Home.

If you know what love is, and if you've had the courage to experience love in its fullness, you will not run away from or fear its intensity. You will go towards it. You will go Home. You will integrate with the fullness of your Self.

In Part Three, the true essence of how you can positively and constructively take responsibility for your actions will be examined, which is an essential part of the ego-death.

PART THREE

CLEARING THE PATHWAY TO BECOMING

The following outlines the experiential ego-death process undertaken at our School of Consciousness. It takes several days to complete, and most of the work on processing and letting go is completed in tutorial ('family') groups.

This work should be done with people you trust to be completely honest with you, who will call you out on your evasive techniques and manipulations, or in other words, those who can bravely hold a mirror up so you can truly see what you have created and begin your journey home to your authentic Self — your Spirit-Self.

I am including this experiential content at this stage to help you understand the remaining concepts presented about karma, the *Bardo*, Renaissance, and Rebirth. I hope that the remaining discussion in this book is less abstract and that, instead, you gain a taste of the Truth through your own direct experience.

 ### FAREWELL LETTERS

Life is a relationship, and you face life's challenges through your intimate connections with others. When the moment arrives to prepare for ego-death, while still living through an old cycle you are trying to terminate, you should sit down and make a list of all the people you love and those you struggle to love. It must include all your important relationships: the easy with the difficult, the happy with the sad, and the fear-filled encounters with those you have in some way offended or couldn't bring yourself to love.

These are the people you have created attachments to: those who have brought meaning to your life, such as your mother, your father, your siblings, your partner, your child, and so on. You should even include those who have brought pain and difficulty to your life because they too have given you opportunities to learn the management of life forces. Each of these people deserves a farewell letter from you, even though nobody but you (and those guiding you in your 'family' group) will ever see what you've written.

When you are genuinely confronted with death, human emotions take precedence. Whatever is undertaken in this light is deeply revealing. This letter-writing exercise addresses the intimate connections between you and those around you and the lessons you have learned from them that deserve acknowledgement.

Ideally, do this exercise with a like-minded and supportive group. If that is not possible, find one person who can act as your letter-writing partner: someone with whom you can be entirely candid, who will listen

When you are genuinely confronted with death, human emotions take precedence. Whatever is undertaken in this light is deeply revealing.

and respond to your strong emotions as you make yourself vulnerable to the addressee of each farewell letter. Best of all would be someone who wants to engage with you by writing their own farewell letters.

The bond between you both should be one of total transparency: your partner should be able to point out any euphemisms, avoidances, embellishments, superficialities, or self-indulgences on your part. In fact, before you start writing, I recommend that you really open up and reveal the tricks, manipulations, and deceptions you habitually employ to avoid full emotional honesty. Ask your partner to help you avoid these old habits.

After writing each letter, read it aloud to your support group or participating partner. Be aware that each reading will require the utmost attention and skill: you must not only listen to the other; you must listen to them *by listening to yourself*. As you share life experiences, you may find yourself deeply moved and feel what your brother or sister feels. And because it is not directly about you, you'll have a better perspective and a broader capacity for understanding, as well as an ability to help the reader.

However, while each letter, like each relationship, is unique, certain habitual patterns tend to repeat in three categories: with loved ones, enemies, and children. Here, you will tend to take sides because, when something really resonates with your experiences, it's hard to see it clearly. That's why a group is better for this process: there is usually one member of this newly formed family who brings a novel perspective. They might pick up on the way you project onto the relative or spouse you idealise, or your deifying of teachers or authority figures. Someone else might perceive how the older sibling tends to be feared or blamed, how often the third or middle sibling tends to be the failure, or how the only child is burdened with a heavy backpack.

It is often easier to achieve take-off in life when your parents throw you out of your home. Alternatively, if your childhood was one of comfort and affection, you can hardly be blamed for never wanting to fly the nest. In the first case, the lesson is obvious: rejection pushes you towards achievement. In the second, you might not understand that comfort and affection can hinder liberation by reducing the challenges that encourage growth. You should thank one for pushing you away and the other for strengthening you so that you can learn the lessons life offers. The former fosters leadership and courage, the latter discernment and serenity.

———

As you share life experiences, you may find yourself deeply moved and feel what your brother or sister feels. And because it is not directly about you, you'll have a better perspective and a broader capacity for understanding, as well as an ability to help the reader.

———

It is hard to separate yourself from those who cover you with the most precious rhinestones and diaphanous veils. Instead of seeing them as they are, you see them as an extension of you. That is why the death of a loved one is so painful: you assume that this person will always be there, that there is no need to tell or show them things that you and they already know. So you never tell them how much you love them or how you appreciate the moments you are with them — and when they are gone, this weighs on you.

It is also difficult to deal naturally with those you consider enemies, traitors, or inferiors when what you want most is to move as far away from them as quickly as possible — or better still, to forget them. It's hard to see something good in someone you consider evil or who caused you pain. Yet these people often teach one of the most important lessons in living, which is to learn forgiveness.

In no case is the mechanism of projection and selfishness as evident as in the parenting of children. Two patterns are observed here, and both demand the re-evaluation of the expression of love. In truth, to love is to see with the eyes of the heart, and of the soul, what is beyond expectations, desires, and proprietary pride.

The first pattern, the most common, involves elevating the child to unrealistic heights, thereby bequeathing them an impossible mission. So intelligence and discernment must be applied. Regardless of their age, you postulate that this letter will be your only verbal legacy, and the child who receives it will be overwhelmed by the sheer weight of responsibility or expectation you've placed on them. No wonder they don't feel seen or understood! Few parents allow themselves to recognise both the virtues and the defects of their children. Already, as a newborn, the nature of a being is grasped, especially by the mother and often by the father, as well. So the parents' job is to mirror their child's real Self, not programme them with their expectations.

The second pattern is less common and requires emotional scrutiny. In this case, the children are viewed with detachment, and usually, one is favoured.

Letter writing is the most important process the School uses for the review and integration of life experiences before dying. It contains all the elements required to rescue life forces misused by undue attachment or exploitation. It shows us to ourselves and to anyone who reads it.

In truth, to love is to see with the eyes of the heart, and of the soul, what is beyond expectations, desires, and proprietary pride.

The content is tangible and straightforward, and you cannot argue with what is written. You cannot mask the implications and say you never meant what is set out in black and white. It stands clear as day and as transparent as when you stand before your own Spirit-Self in death. Both the writing process and the finished letter reveal who and what you are.

The instructions given at the School are specific. A letter always has a purpose, and this farewell letter is about severing from the past. It must be definitive. It must contain truths that, whether good or unpleasant, cause emotional pain. It must undo the knots of selfishness and possession. It must liberate the writer and the person to whom it is written. Letters are very different from speaking on the telephone or even face to face. To formulate the message, you must think, feel, and find the appropriate words, images, and details that bestow meaning to the communication. So, when writing a farewell letter, you are forced to relive the relationship at a subtle level, fully awakening the body's memory, the emotional content, and the mental implications.

Here, every word counts, and the participation of each member of the small 'family' group created for the processing of the letters must fully understand, see, and experience the relationship. The addressee becomes real in front of every member of the group, immersed in the unfolding drama as before a gripping movie. If the communication is deemed real, deep, and complete with details and memories, it is found satisfactory. If it holds back in any way (usually due to the emotional difficulty of having to sever a powerful bond) or if it is filled with recriminations and accusations, or if it promises eternal ties of undying affection or veiled threats echoing persistently hurt feelings — if any of these inauthentic ideas are expressed, it is rewritten again and again. This continues until it is devoid of egoism and the writer can stand in dignity and integrity with their letter as a monument to an experience fully lived and a life lesson learned.

Throughout our lives, we experience innumerable dramas that we carry within us, some enacted repeatedly, some stored away, yet to be acknowledged, and others lying in wait to be lived. Death is a moment when nothing is left unseen or pending. So each new redraft of a letter offers a revelation, and those who thought they had understood everything about themselves are the soonest to be surprised.

When a letter is first written, only surface imprints or emotions are exposed. But with each new version, the writer must inquire more deeply into the hidden impressions that spice the undercurrents of the relationship, and in doing so, they can awaken surprising insights. That is the purpose of the exercise. It can be hard to guess how many rewrites are required for each relationship left behind — as few as five, perhaps, or as many as twenty — until finally, in that last letter, the writer can release the person and the dramas that link them together. And this is achieved with the impartiality, appreciation, and gratitude demanded by the process.

It is hard to let go of difficult relationships that involve forgiveness, especially when addressing enemies, whether declared or implied. These letters require you to change perspective and view the relationship from other angles that enable neutrality and fairness. In other words, you need to let go of gripes. It is even harder to release love relationships that bind you in blood ties or lifelong partnerships — and it's almost unbearable to write farewell letters to small children.

Crucially, all our letters require the final seal irradiated by the person's conscience when viewed from the 'top'. This is our terminology for standing aside from the personality and incorporating the perspective of the Spirit-Self. The reader may find it difficult to understand, but this is not a mere mental attitude. It's a radical energy *Gestalt* that prevails at the higher dimensions of Being. It is acquired through the practice of the *Alchemical Alignment*. This view from the top is what links us to all spiritual traditions and is the very purpose of the process.

Needless to say, leaving the safehouse of our habits and predispositions does not please the personality, which will not happily relinquish the juicy bone of meaning and self-importance, the grudges or vows made, the situations it could not control or the obstacles that took it on a detour from its desires. But this is all part of the letter-writing sessions at the School, which can last from a full week to ten days.

As happens when recalling unfortunate situations in childhood — the silent suffering, the secret betrayals — one asks, 'Why bring this up *now*?' or, 'Why remember something that is no longer applicable and where the person has changed?' Our answer is, 'Because those imprints are, in part, repressed sentient energy and remain encapsulated in the nervous system, preventing the free circulation of sensibility needed for the full expression of Love. You recognise those blocked feelings in concealed memories hampering the depth and expansiveness of the mind at all

> These letters require you to change perspective and view the relationship from other angles that enable neutrality and fairness.

levels, especially the highest spiritual realm where intensities of grace, joy, and ecstasy require the tolerance and sustaining power of a lucid, stable, integrated personality'.

As you go through the following letters written by students at our School, dear reader, bear in mind the stirrings of the heart prevailing in each of them. Don't just read them as you would an ordinary text. Listen. Feel. Sense the moisture in the eyes of the writer and the soft, often choking, sobbing tone of the voice that says farewell to a very precious part of their deeply human life.

The following letters are divided into two sections: incomplete and complete. After each letter is a description of why it was found to be incomplete or why it was deemed complete. Former students kindly agreed to share these deeply personal letters with you as an act of service — so that you may gain insight into both the extreme difficulty and the deep joy of letting go of the ego, and connecting with and embodying your true Self.

INCOMPLETE LETTERS

The first letters below illustrate the process and some of the blocks that students face in truly letting go. These include letters to a younger sibling, a mother, an adoptive father, a son, a couple to each other, and a husband to his wife.

Letter to a younger sibling

My Sweet Little Sister,

I'm writing to you because my life is about to end. I have very little time left to tell you how much you meant to me. I had come into the world earlier in a country and at a moment in its history that marked great change. I didn't have much time to enjoy my parents' exclusive attention and love, because seven months later you were already in our mother's belly. I was 18 months old when you showed up. Mom tried to prepare me for this, as she thought it would help me to be ready to share everything with you. At that time, I was still too young to understand what it meant to 'have' something, to truly 'give'. So, I was given my role, which I (probably) wasn't ready for developmentally. In our house's reward and punishment system, I had to be specially rewarded when I was 'good' to you and punished when I was 'unkind'. That's probably why I've learned to expect an extra reward from those around me and I have become demanding, mostly from you. I expected you to play with me and do as I said.

You were a 'war child'. Mom was so scared of the outbreak of martial law that she gave birth to you a few weeks ahead of schedule. Your life has been marked by her fear. Your separation from the safety of her belly was premature. That's why you cried so much; you were very sensitive and you didn't want to eat. Unfortunately, circumstances put you in a nursery, which only made your traumas worse. I suspect that your spirit was already severely broken by then, which later affected the development of your spine, and you had severe scoliosis. Jumping off Grandma's balcony didn't help either.

We were both sensitive in our own way, but I suspect my manner of expression must have often overwhelmed you. I could be loud and aggressive. I treated you as a part of me because we never had a chance to be separate. We did everything together, but I was older, so it's obvious that some things I could do better. It made me feel unnecessarily proud and arrogant because I knew everything better than you. We had different talents — I was a humanist and you were better at science. It is clearly visible in the paths we have chosen.

We had a great time together. We had cool ideas and space in the garden to build our bases in the bushes, decorate a beauty salon with flower petals, and spend a lot of time in nature. I remember how funnily you twisted words, that you were talking in your sleep, your abstract sense of humour. We had some common interests, mainly music. Our cassette player was our special treasure. Our playlist from that period is all classics today. When we were 12 and 13 years old, we became Girl Scouts, and that became our common reference for many years. You supported my ideas and were my faithful sidekick. We could trust each other then. But life did not stand still.

Growing up changed our bodies and complicated our relationships. I distanced myself from you when I fell in love with B. It had the effect of breaking up the scout team. You had difficulties in high school with that mean language teacher. Your scoliosis got worse, and you had to go to rehabilitation for many months. You were told that if you ever got pregnant, you'd have to lie down all the time.

I treated you as a part of me because we never had a chance to be separate.

It must have affected you because you never started a family. When I left for college, you were left alone with our parents and moved to a new house. You must have worked very hard back then. I never thanked you. I was already too engrossed in my new life in the capital. Then the greatest tragedy of our lives happened, and it affected you the most: our father's death. I'm so sorry for what you went through. Such pain is hard to bear and hard to recover from. I know you're healing just now.

Your first college cost you a lot of stress. Then you chose medicine, and it was better. There you met G. When my husband appeared, I almost completely disappeared. My pregnancy shocked you. Our whole world suddenly changed. You must have felt betrayed and abandoned by me. I wasn't thinking about you at all, focused on my thesis and my new life with him. I needed you then, but it was too much for you to handle. It took us a while to get over our emotions in this situation. I don't think you knew how to act. You and G lived near us at the time, but we rarely met. You didn't want to interfere and probably learned not to take responsibility for my life.

You were writing your bachelor's degree then; you were changing your studies and you were starting to think about a doctorate. Then your husband was your main support, your big teddy bear to cuddle with. He accepted you as you were. You didn't have to adjust to me anymore. I was a young mother preoccupied with my new child. You must have had a hard time adjusting to it all. You tried your best, but I guess you felt that there was no place for you in my life anymore.

My move to the countryside was another stage of separation for us. I see clearly now how different we are — we have different talents, different needs, and even our nervous systems differ in how they regulate. We have chosen different paths, and we both developed the gifts we received from our parents in some way. Even your move to Australia, the country Dad was so impressed with, is not accidental. I became a mother and put down roots. You travelled the world on business and privately. I'm sorry that I expected you to be like me, to want to share my values and lifestyle. Thank you for your presence in my children's lives. They know that they can always call you and visit you in the beautiful place where you live now. I'm sorry I tried to manipulate you and emotionally blackmail you with my situations.

You had no obligation to take care of my family. I see your beauty, your courage to go into the unknown and to persevere and carry the burden of your/our trauma. Maybe, if I were you, I wouldn't be able to handle it, but you still manage to keep the joyfulness of a child.

I wasn't the best sister that I thought I was. I nurtured this delusion as part of my identity. In fact, I often hurt you and ignored your needs. I always had to be right and have the last word. Who was I to impose anything on you? My arrogance and superiority prevented me from seeing you for real. You were my mirror, and our life together with all its difficult moments allowed me to discover who I really am. I bow to you, dear sister, for this. I've learned so much from you. My greatest lesson is humility and the recognition that I can't control anyone. That was my disrespect to you. I'm sorry with all my heart. We are equal. We both have our light. I need to go now. I just love you. Farewell.

Your Older Sister,

K.

In this letter to a sister, notice the typical characteristics displayed between siblings, especially those of the same gender. In particular, there's the hesitancy to say anything harsh or hurtful, a reluctance everyone feels when first attempting to write letters of this type and raise what was previously left unsaid. The reason for this usually lies with emotions, but now, as the individual stands naked before the mirror of their life, all these issues arise in order to be embraced by Consciousness.

In this letter, it turns out that the 'sweet little sister' might not have been as sweet as the writer wants to believe, though there's no way to know for sure. Her phrases are laced with doubt and wishful thinking. Note how often she writes 'probably' or 'I guess' or 'I'm sorry', excusing her sister's actions and presumed attitude and taking all the blame upon herself.

She is quite hard on herself at the end, but there is no way to 'spare the whip' if you wish to express yourself with clarity, understanding, and above all, compassion. This is the hallmark of the neophyte. It marks the shift from looking outward and being hopelessly at the mercy of the external world, to looking inward at the self as the cause. Within the School, we know that, in time, this intensity will relax to the point where

—

As the individual stands naked before the mirror of their life, all these issues arise in order to be embraced by Consciousness.

—

she will no longer feel remorse but embrace herself as she is — not good or bad, just human. For now, though, her feelings of goodwill are enough to release her from the negativity of the past, but not enough to truly release her from the past.

Letter to a mother

Hi Mummy,

Thank you for being my mum, the best one I could have here. I know that you have loved me very much. I was your long-awaited child. Even my great-grandmother sewed me a quilt that I used as a pillow throughout my childhood. It's because of you that our house was a safe space. Despite hard times, you were able to give me a colourful world of fairy tales and games. I remember how you played with me, made up games, and let me play on my own. You cared about boundaries and rules; their awareness planted then has stayed with me to this day. You cooked well, and thanks to you, I got to know the 'taste of life' — your amazing cookies and cakes, although as a child, I was picky. It was very hard for me to do things under duress. For eating, going to church, doing things not my tempo but under your command or emotional blackmail. I really admired your wide reading and intelligence; you had amazing knowledge and unimaginable memory for facts and dates. I know that you were a natural-born teacher from a teachers' family. But sometimes there was tension when you and Daddy were fighting. I was so terrified then. The word divorce became the scariest thing in the world. That's why I never married.

Our relationship deteriorated when I started puberty. I felt unaccepted, ugly, and lost. I didn't get on well in school with my peers, and when Emma bullied me, I was not prepared for the cruelty and I couldn't protect myself. You probably didn't understand my sensitivity and my longing for acceptance from my peers. We were fighting very badly at that time.

You never crossed my boundaries. Instead, you delegated to Dad for that. He was punishing me on your behalf. I felt terrible about that; I was afraid of him, and I lost my trust in you. Physical punishment was anguish and big trauma; I felt that it was so unfair and too much. In fact, I was a good girl. Polite, a talented student, and a loving daughter. I know that you made an effort. You gave me birthday parties and Christmas presents, but the only thing that I missed was the feeling that you really saw me. Your attitude towards your own body made me feel that my body is irrelevant/ugly. I got the feeling that you didn't support the awakening of my femininity, on physical and emotional levels. It seemed to me that you completely ignored your (and therefore my) gender.

There were some good sides — you were discreet, and you never asked about intimate details of my life. I felt there was no space for such topics between us. I didn't know how I looked because you never related to my appearance. I felt unattractive because we never had nice clothes or cosmetics. Even when I desperately needed them for my acne, you didn't understand my shame and you didn't take care of it. I had to learn from others how to be a woman. I started to despise you for your bad taste and how you didn't care for yourself.

You were always busy with school and checking on homework; you didn't like music (I guess you were overwhelmed) but you supported my writing. You checked my essays and seemed to approve. But I really didn't like that you read my diary; my awkward poems were my secret. I had a feeling that we didn't have much in common; we had different sensitivities and interests. Sometimes your behaviour and your acts made me feel ashamed of you when I was looking at you through the eyes of a teenager. Today I think that you were a volcano of energy, raising two children, taking care of the house and our little garden, and coping with the grey reality of that time.

You have been wishing me all the best and you were proud of me, especially when I passed my final exams and went to college in America. Then, when you bought the house with Dad, it seemed that everything was going right, but suddenly, out of the blue, he died, killed himself. That broke our hearts. We stayed alone, us three, condemned to each other, with the perspective of your lonely life in the new house. I know that the circumstances brought us together, this despair and emptiness we experienced each in our own way. Since then I was supposed to take care of Agnes, to be 'smarter' because 'I'm older'. I had to share everything with her and give in to her on everything. This is how it was; we shared a room; we had

Holy Communion together; shared clothes. This situation made me responsible, always taking care of others. I was giving; she was receiving; this is how you raised us. I felt it was unfair somehow. My sister could be unbearable, but I was the one punished, spanked, and teased. Something went wrong. I could hurt you many times as an impulsive teenager, mouthy and angry whenever I felt that you were imposing something on me, but you didn't appreciate my effort; you didn't understand who I am.

Everything changed when I got pregnant. This is my favourite chapter of our relationship. From the moment you found out that you were going to be a grandma, you changed. I'm so, so grateful for your support, care, and absolute love for Laura, even when she was in my belly. You were the greatest grandma, and I have never forgotten that. Maybe it was because you had more time then, but everything you were doing for us was full of love, and I have felt it every time we have visited you. You were able to enjoy your grandchildren so much and so wonderfully. Although sometimes I felt like there was some pressure to make us happy by force, I appreciate your presence in my family's life, your full acceptance of my decisions, and no pressure on marriage. You were always ready to support us, whenever it was needed. Sometimes we didn't agree. You always 'knew better', unfortunately.

I'm so proud of you for how you have organised your retirement and how you have moved the university for seniors into our hometown, for so many people. You were always an activist and a fine organiser. You hiked more than I probably ever will. You just loved to fool around and laugh; you were amazingly creative and brave. You could do a lot for others, but you have respected your boundaries. My kids just adored you.

When the pandemic started, you panicked. As usual, there was a lot of hysteria, and the situation was uncertain then for us all. When it seemed that the disease was subsiding, you took the risky decision (you didn't have time to get vaccinated) of going to the mountains with your friends. There you got Covid. I know that you were bored and lonely at home and so stubborn that I didn't even try to discuss it.

The last time we saw each other was a month before you died. I'm so happy that I could hug you then and eat your amazing cooking.

Mom, I'm so sorry that you were there completely alone. I hope that there were angels around you. The helplessness of old age… I'm so sorry I wasn't there next to you. Thank you for all you have taught me: first of all, to be a strong, intelligent, resourceful, open-minded, and caring woman. What I didn't get from you, I learned from others, and I know you have learned from me.

I love you.

Y.

Letters to mothers are especially archetypal, particularly those from a female child to her mother.

Observe the placating tone of this letter. It transmits the clichés universally expected in our society: to always be self-observant, caring, and, above all, considerate of those around oneself. This is especially so in the case of a mother, who must always be deemed sacred, no matter her behaviour towards her child in the past. So deeply ingrained is our universal heritage that it's difficult to find a living person who does not carry some guilt about not loving a parent as they 'should'.

I present this letter as a 'best as can be' example written by a well-integrated member of a country deeply embedded in Christianity. While we respect this attitude in our school, we cannot help but notice the sense of obligation and the conciliatory language that reveal an impenetrable layer of indoctrination, usually to the detriment of self-esteem. It was written by someone deeply observant of cultural expectations in a prosperous but nonetheless traditional European country.

Her mother's memory is a source of unfinished business for her and will undoubtedly show up a little in her relationships with the elderly or mother figures. Although the love for her mother is genuine, it echoes one of the Ten Commandments: 'Honour your father and your mother', to which may be appended 'even if they are less than honourable'. This last comment may sound insensitive when not considering the energetic personal and self-derogatory implications beneath the use of words — all too evident in this particular case.

A lot of the previous rewriting of this letter had to do with the student's insistence on excusing her mother's actions, time and again, much as a child does when they whisper to themselves, 'But Mommy loves me anyway!' She claims that her mother treated her and her sister equally, but it seems apparent to all that she did not. In fact, she was as incapable of defending her inner child back then as she is today.

Whenever she pointed out instances of her mother not understanding her, she immediately followed up with, 'But I didn't understand myself either!' As if this were an obligation on her own part and a requirement towards gaining her mother's understanding. She even goes so far as to expect the impossible of herself as a child when she says, 'I couldn't appreciate your support then'. This remains disguised self-blame. In some other aspects of the work on the Self and Consciousness, in direct alignment with her soul, she will undoubtedly achieve the rightful release in love and the influx of self-worth due to her.

Letter from a daughter to her adoptive father

Dear Dad,

This is the last time we will speak, and I want to express what our relationship has meant to me.

You are not my biological father and you have never met my expectations of what a father should be. It felt like I was growing up in a family of strangers. I was an imposter but needed a father so badly. The lack of love, attention, and affection has had a profound effect on my life thus far, as I can see how my childhood experiences have shaped my personality so that I can appear hard and defensive today. You were never there. I don't forgive you for not being there. WHERE WERE YOU? I needed you and it hurt badly when you deprived me of love.

I always felt that you should have fully embraced and understood the complexities of the responsibility you were taking on before you and Mum adopted me. You couldn't have your own biological child and that must have made you resent my being someone else's flesh and blood. I felt that. It must have been a massive blow and disappointment, making you feel unworthy.

'Unavailable' is the word I would use to describe you during my early life. You were a workaholic and fully-functioning alcoholic choosing whiskey as company rather than me in your spare time. To start with, I wanted your attention; I wanted you to love me because, when I had it, you could be fun. You were at your best when watching musicals, and that was the only time I ever saw any type of emotion. You always cried at the end of *Showboat*, and I found this endearing and beautifully human. However, your strong opinions shadowed this and were always delivered with force and a sense of authority. As a teenager, I started to disagree with your views and was often met with indignance and force rather than curiosity. I hated you for this and rebelled by shutting you out. I am sorry that we were not able to talk and that, for most of my teen years, we ended up shouting at each other. I really needed you to help me navigate through life, but time and time again, you ignored me, and we were unable to connect.

I watched as you bullied Mum and made your demands, which she complied with. This helped form my unhealthy opinion of what men were like. My respect for you ebbed away and was replaced with contempt.

There were moments of joy when we were in Wales on holiday and you would host sports days for all the children on the beach. That was my fun dad, that was who I wanted to have all the time. But he was not available for the most part, and that was a second blow of abandonment for me.

One moment had a huge impact on my journey. It was the day I came to tell you that I had an interview for a management position at a prestigious media company. I was 22. You told me not to expect anything, that I wouldn't get the job because I was inexperienced and probably not up to it. This was a pivotal moment; I thought, 'Fuck you, I'll show you', and I did. But I was still looking for your approval; I guess I still am. This moment made me question authority and opinions, not take everything I was told as gospel, challenge the status quo, and have belief in my inner voice. What a gift you gave me as these traits have helped me with the determination that has driven me through my life; a great lesson and without sarcasm, I honestly thank you.

As we are both at the end of our lives; we have tried to settle our differences and develop a better relationship. I have never considered you as my father; I'm sorry but I haven't. However, you are an exceptional grandparent to my children, and they love you deeply. And I love the 'Pops' you have been for them. They have had the best of you.

I understand that you were not held or loved fully as a child and that our relationship has been affected by this. As the only child of loveless, controlling parents growing up on the wrong side of Manchester, you came to be my parent with your own trauma. I have learned that your lack of emotion and connection does not mean you don't care for or love me; you just don't know how to show love. I know now that you love me in your own way. I can see the lost boy in you and have huge compassion for the lack of love you were given. I see you clearly now; I see your pain, your desire to connect, but how lost you are when attempting to. You never knew love; how could you give it? How could you connect to me when you were not connected to your Self?

I will leave, carrying pain and grief from our relationship with acceptance that it is what it is and that you did the best you could.

With love,

V.

The language in this letter barely masks the blame and anger, eventually leading to the admission that she has felt 'contempt' for this father. She makes little effort to disguise her disappointment in him and in what she recognises as a continuing need for his approval and appreciation. But she did not go deeply enough into her own pain to go beyond it into release and forgiveness.

While shedding uncomfortable truths about him, she also puts down her mother, revealing little understanding or compassion. The wounds caused by her birth abandonment remain as vivid as ever: raw emotions armed in adulthood by a razor-sharp mind. The sarcasm she employs is not dissipated when she qualifies his behaviour towards her as a 'gift' that has given her the determination and power to drive through life's difficulties. Admitting that this was a 'great lesson' does not veil the fact that she appears to be mentally (and somewhat prematurely) forcing out words of forgiveness without experiencing their meaning deeply within. Sarcasm coats contempt.

Especially revealing in this letter is another of today's common characteristics when well-meaning people convince themselves that they have forgiven someone. They arm themselves with psychological tools to foster a rational understanding that does not resonate with the emotions or the body. Here, she skilfully concludes that her father is like he is because of early childhood trauma. On the same note, at the very end, she bids her farewell, saying, 'You did the best you could'. This sounds like condescension.

Unfortunately, her 'understanding' sounds hollow when she asks rhetorically, 'How could you connect to me when you were not connected to your Self?' This assumes a spiritual superiority that masks a profound lack of humility. The lines where she refers to him as 'Pops' and praises him for being a good grandfather to her children don't quite succeed in balancing out the former part of the letter in either length or tone.

Why say 'nasty' things? Only when the child is allowed to speak as it truly feels in the past, and not with the understanding of the present, will the energy encapsulated by pain be released. At this stage, she covers her pain with anger and never goes deeper.

Knowing this woman as I do, her adoption remains a big unresolved issue for the simple reason that it was an extremely intense experience received at a pre-verbal stage before the infant has any opportunity to understand or relate to its environment. To use psychological terminology again, this largely accounts for her volatile temperament and defensive-accusatory tone. It will take a lot of patience and courage for her to go deeply 'into that dark night' alone so she can embrace it and emerge in a spirit of genuine forgiveness and self-worth. But I am certain she will.

Letter from a mother to her son

Matt,

Saying goodbye to you is unbearable, but I feel that it's important that I leave having told you what you mean to me and how you have brought so much love and learning to my life.

You are my firstborn, my son. I used to say that you would be a footballer when you grow up, given the active kicking you did when I carried you. I loved you so much before I met you; you were so wanted. I remember my excitement while painting fish and sharks on your nursery walls; I was so thrilled about your arrival. Even before you were born, you taught me how to love unconditionally and brought patience, balance, and peace to my life. Four weeks after you were born, I remember dancing on Christmas morning to Nat

> Only when the child is allowed to speak as it truly feels in the past, and not with the understanding of the present, will the energy encapsulated by pain be released.

King Cole with you asleep in my arms. I didn't think I could love you more… but I could, and I did, and I do.

As a young boy, you were loving and affectionate. I showered you with hugs and loved making sure I gave you what I hadn't had. I hope I didn't smother you too much, although I suspect I did. I hope you felt the love I had for you then and all through your life so far. On reflection, though, I can see how I must have projected my abandonment fears on you and never left your side and constantly worried something might happen to you. I felt real fear for the first time ever and developed an overactive need to protect. I can now see that this was restrictive and *controlling*, and I'm sorry for needing you too much.

From an early age, you had a keen interest in aquatic life, particularly sharks, and an unusual passion for environmental issues. You developed strong ethics and morals that made and still make me proud of you. You caused me little trouble and were a joy to be around, a popular, sporty boy who had good manners and great conversation. Although a little shy, your confidence has grown with age.

You are now a man at 18 years old and I could not be prouder. But I understand that is part of my ego showing off that you met my expectations. You have become, for the most part, what my idea of a good son should be. On occasions, when you don't meet my expectations, I come down hard, and I am truly sorry for this. I could not see how my expectations and control were suffocating. I do not own you, and I am sorry if you felt the weight of my parenting style.

I am also sorry for how the divorce affected you; I broke the strong bond of trust we had previously taken for granted. I know that you don't fully understand why I did what I did, but I want you to know that nothing was your fault, and the three of you were the best thing that ever happened to me. I can see how my fear of losing you during the last few years has made me manipulate situations so that you would favour me over your dad. I was so scared of what the divorce would do to you that I controlled and lied about things to try to protect you from hurting. I should have trusted you more, as you can make your own decisions, the ones that are right for you, not what I perceive to be right.

I know that our relationship has changed recently as I try to guide you as best I can. This can also come out as me making demands caused by past patterns I carry, and sometimes my guidance can be selfish and not what is necessarily best for you. We have had fights over our differences of opinions, and you hurt me deeply with your cutting words of punishment. But it is my fault for putting my own fears on you like shackles. No wonder you want to break free.

I want to take this opportunity to tell you that I do trust that you will make the right decisions going forward. This is your journey and I want to give you my blessing for you to run your life as you see fit. I see your wisdom. I see your pain. I see what I have put on you, and I free you from any responsibility.

You are so wise and kind, strong and courageous, funny and sweet. You have taught me to question my motivation and not project my fears onto you. You have taught me discernment. You call me out and hold me accountable all the time, and I am so grateful, even if I don't show it.

You are 6 feet 5 inches tall, but you are still my little boy. You have taught me that you were never really 'mine'. You have not inherited many of my unconscious behaviours. You are aware of my patterns. Keep your awareness. You are your own person. Always be guided by your instinct; you can trust it. Go inside and you will find the answer.

You are loved. You are loveable. I respect you. It was an absolute privilege to be a part of your journey. You are not alone.

Darling boy,

Mum x

As evidenced by the profusion of 'sorry', her repetition of 'fear', and specifically the phrase 'you hurt me deeply', she puts herself on an even level with her child.

There is no liberation. Parents' letters to their children are invariably painful to write, read, or receive, filled as they often are with projections and regret — too much of this, too little of that — and cushioned with self-love and vicarious pride in the child's achievements. A mother's letter is predictably exaggerated, revealing a particular brand of possessiveness.

To believe that a child (or anyone) can bring patience, balance, and peace is unrealistic. Furthermore, it is something that the child is apt to believe and to attribute to the parent's needs rather than to their own inherent nature. Patience, balance, and peace are achieved through the *experience* of being a parent, especially during motherhood, which requires a lifelong energetic womb connection with the being who has grown within. These virtues are an essential part of the mother's learning that she should apply to the rest of her life rather than use as a badge for herself or her child. It is unrealistic to think that anyone, even your own child, can *bring* you love if you have none. Love should be learned so that it can manifest through the presence and interaction with a vulnerable dependent. We are not talking about 'goods' to be obtained or bestowed, but something that arises from within.

Mothers are notably overpowering and possessive in their sometimes desperate attempt to give their children the goods and opportunities they never had. The fear of loss of appreciation dominates the relationship. Mothers also tend to emote over the idea of a good son or daughter, as in this letter, extending undue appreciation for good behaviour rather than the unique inherent traits of their offspring, which they often do not notice or understand. Very little is seen of her son in this letter, except at the very end, where she falsely releases him from any responsibilities (meaning guilt) he might feel to her in future.

This letter shows the force of manipulation under the guise of protectiveness — a common characteristic in all forms of person-to-person human affection. It also illustrates the unconscious swings between affection, reprimand, demonstrations of approval, and guilty compensation.

When she accepts that she and her son have had differences that she is glad about, she follows that with 'you hurt me deeply'. These are words that place guilt upon him yet again. It is a wobbly posture, never being straight with him, always defending herself and then asking for forgiveness while affirming that she does trust him.

Nonetheless, there is a real feeling of sincerity and genuine hope that he can find himself and succeed in life. She is giving the best advice she could, something he could keep with him if the letter had been a real legacy left to him upon her death.

Parents' letters to their children are invariably painful to write, read, or receive, filled as they often are with projections and regret and cushioned with self-love and vicarious pride in the child's achievements.

LETTERS BY A COUPLE

Letter from a woman to her partner

My Dearest,

All that I lacked I found in you. I loved you as best I could and purified myself in you. All the good moments were expressed on your face in the form of smiles, and how beautiful those smiles were, what good they did me! However, when you were angry, how difficult it was to tolerate your temperamental outbursts! How many times have we had to solve, in a single day, an endless number of problems and arguments? I would say that all that might have been a waste of time if it had not helped our love to mature.

My love was always growing, despite the doubt that you were the ideal woman to share my life with forever. I was always very fickle. And the traumas, grudges, resentments, and your bad temper wore me out a lot. The predicaments we got into were not the easiest. Even the love affairs were a bit risky. I remember when we spent that weekend alone in that apartment, loving each other, feeling each other, touching each other. It was beautiful!

I know I made many mistakes and that I have many flaws, but I think we would make a perfect couple. I will carry you in my memory. I was impregnated with your presence in this life, and I want to carry this bond of love beyond death. Be happy, love yourself, go with God. I love you and I will always love you madly.

Always yours.

Notice how this letter does *not* release the partner and ends with promises of hope. However, now to her partner's letter:

My companion, my lover, my friend:

You were, for a long time, part of my being. How you completed me! How much we learned together! How much expansion, how much love! Your happiness was always synonymous with mine. We made many mistakes, I admit it. There were many scenes of jealousy. How many wasted tears, how many fights! However, despite that, every fight, every tear, every smile was followed by a lesson. I thank you so much for all the learning. I thank you for the love you gave me. You will never leave my essence, as I hope not to leave yours.

Now our paths are parting. I make one last request: be happy and live fully. Give yourself to others as you did to me so that they can learn with you as I was able to learn with you. Promise me that you will take care of yourself, because only then will I be able to go in peace. Never think of me with sadness, for I want to be a beautiful memory in your life, as you are in mine.

I love you and I will continue to love you wherever I am, and I will be happy knowing that I had the chance to feel how great a feeling of love can be. Go with God and try not to be discouraged by the sadness of our separation. Nothing between us is loss because we only gain from our relationship. Take with you all my love and heart.

Kisses from who was only yours.

Many couples, such as this, come together on this plane to complete a part of themselves instead of being whole within themselves. This is a simple but disguised exploitation. They do not realise that the other is merely serving as a mirror, and that what attracted them were the qualities manifested by the other or projected onto them, aspects that the individual already possessed and was trying to express.

You cannot keep a part of the other or leave a part of yourself in them. They are *they* and you are *you*. If you are unaware of this, you are using it as a crutch, and you will never really recognise and love your partner for what they are but for what they give you. Mature love is about recognising the moment of meeting and the moment of parting, not trying to take a part of the other that does not belong to you.

True love, mature and self-conscious, knows that on the physical plane, nothing is eternal and that one cannot pretend to transport energies to other dimensions without alchemically transmuting them.

Transmutation is only possible when there is a total and unconditional opening of hands: a total renunciation of the possession or perpetuation of egoic emotions. This is one of the purposes of ego-death while living.

Relationships of all types provide the basic learning ground (one could say 'battleground') in life, as in spiritual development. None is more intense

---

You cannot keep a part of the other or leave a part of yourself in them. They are they and you are you. If you are unaware of this, you are using it as a crutch, and you will never really recognise and love your partner for what they are but for what they give you.

---

than the relationship within a couple, where instinctual sexual fire ignites not only the physical but also the mental and, especially, emotional energies.

In our school, during the death process, relationship letters serve to illustrate patterns bequeathed by parents and ancestors, a legacy of pain and often violence engraved upon cellular memory. People rarely see one another devoid of the filter of their projection, so it is significant that, in our experience, couples sometimes break up after this process, recognising that what they called love was projection, need, or fear. Other couples return to one another considerably more lucid and committed to taking the spiritual path together. Such was the culmination of the letter shown below, in the beginning stages of blame and pain (that, in truth, had nothing to do with one or the other). Fortunately, both partners were in the process, so both sides could be followed impartially. Here is only his side, which is enough to illustrate what happens in life and what might happen when they awaken beyond the subliminal memories helplessly embedded in their bodies.

Many of us believe our romantic love relationships to be our most important. Here is one more example of an incomplete letter by a husband to his wife.

L is especially passionate, highly intelligent, and intense; possibly, he is the more insecure and obsessively romantic Latin Lover. She is equally intense, beautiful, striking, proud, and obviously aware of her grip over him — a proud, warrior-like but suffering heroine. Together they have travelled the world over.

Letter from a husband to his wife

My Love,

I don't even know where to start this letter. I never envisioned this as a possibility, but the truth is, I am dying. I am haunted by the thought that I couldn't make you happy. You always told me that you felt invisible to me, accusing me, 'With everyone but not with me'. Yet, the heartbreaking truth is I never betrayed you, not even in thought.

It felt like you blamed me for your father's absence. You yearned to be the center of my universe; if a moment passed without my reply, an accusation followed. Every time I voiced an opinion, you took it personally. Expressing my disagreements or dislikes became a reason for you to feel attacked or hurt. If I ever raised my voice in anger, you were swift to scold, as though only you held that right. But, of course, you never admitted this. This was the price I paid for your brother's actions too, labelled as violent, and it made me feel like a wretched abuser.

I was like a father to your daughters, supporting them, providing what they needed. Yet, if I ever expressed my discontent with their behaviour, especially with the eldest, you'd say that if I didn't love her, I didn't love you either. But, notice this, due to my strictness, she sought help, moved out, and learned responsibility.

You've endlessly expressed feeling unsupported. I've confronted your daughters, asking them to help you more, reminding them of your sacrifices for them. Yet, when I stood up for you, you'd get mad at me for intervening.

You always lamented my lack of affection. My love, it was you who taught me to embrace and be embraced. For me, loving you meant catering to your desires, being a provider, and ensuring our children's education. Ironically, what I criticised my father for, I ended up replicating. I'm sorry; I struggled to act differently, and whenever I tried, my inability to articulate my sadness angered me. I felt inadequate and feared that you'd leave me. I'd get defensive, shout and then be consumed by guilt and remorse, chastising myself for repeating my father's mistakes.

You've always expressed feeling alone, and I'd wonder: what more could I do? All I did was work tirelessly for our family: for you, your daughters, my children, and our shared child.

You always wished for sweet words. Damn! I just didn't know how. I showed my love by being intimate with only you. And every time you lamented my lack of verbal affection, I felt inadequate, reminiscent of my childhood feelings with my parents.

I felt hurt when you suspected I could betray you. Your unfounded jealousy upset me, especially since I rarely noticed when someone flirted with me. It made me feel naïve and, at the same time, frantic.

Every argument somehow circled back to my ex-wife. I never understood why you felt that way, accusing me of still loving her, not realising that it's you I've loved the most.

I've been by your side during the tough times: raising your daughters, through your mother's illness and issues with your siblings. I asked you to set boundaries, but you didn't, and our son and I took a back seat. Your stress and compulsiveness only grew. You never had a moment of peace, always busying yourself, and if I ever voiced my concerns you'd say I didn't understand. I didn't marry you for a housekeeper; I wanted a partner. I yearned for moments with you, doing nothing, just feeling your presence.

I wished for you to let go, to moan with pleasure when we made love, instead of worrying if we'd be heard. So? Why did it matter if they heard us?

Despite constantly supporting and encouraging your personal and professional growth, you felt I didn't value you. To me, assisting your growth was an act of love.

Gratitude from you scared me. Firstly, because I wasn't used to being thanked, and, secondly, fearing you'd later blame me for my shortcomings.

You accused me of not spending time with our son, echoing my own mother's words, 'Your Dad is very good'. You portrayed me as absent and uninvolved, making me feel like a failing father. You worried excessively about potential harms, overprotecting him. I was the 'bad cop', you the 'good cop'.

With our plans to move countries, I felt that you left me behind. Was it fear or was it the old dynamics with your family? I felt deserted, undervalued, and insufficient.

Look at what I've done again. Bark like Pekas, our dog, the one you picked up from the streets. You know, I feel like him. I came into your life wounded, and with your love I healed and stood tall. I've been fierce in defending what I believe is mine, but deep down I'm just a vulnerable pup who felt safe by your side.

In truth, we're like two injured dogs who found each other to heal mutual wounds. Sometimes, the healing hurt, and we'd bark and scare each other.

Forgive me for raising my voice, for any hurt I might have caused, for making you feel less. My sole wish in life was to see you happy. Now I understand that it wasn't in my control but yours. I saw in you my relationship with my mother.

You can't fathom how much I've loved you. I discovered love in your embrace, your kisses, your touch. With you, I could be me. You knew everything about me; I had no secrets. Inside you, I felt manly, sufficient, complete. Every venture in my life included you; I always sought your opinion. I always believed we could achieve anything together.

You've been the only one, the real one. You found your way into my heart, like a drip that eventually broke down my walls.

Why do I love you? Because I choose to. Being loyal to you was never an obligation but a genuine desire. I love your sensitivity. You've been a salve for this wounded warrior. I cherish your innocence, that complete woman who is also a defenceless child at times. You are like the phoenix, rising from its ashes, or the lotus flower that blooms amidst the mud.

I'll cherish our joyous moments, our intimacy, not just our sexuality, which was delightful, but our soulful encounters too. I'll remember our midnight talks, post-lovemaking, about you, me, and us, whether they were profound or mere whimsies. I'll treasure our moments, accompanied by wine, cheese, and candlelight. We didn't need much to enjoy each other.

Sharing my life with you around the world has been an honour. It's been enthralling to seek our essence together. It's impossible not to envision us exploring the universe in pursuit of truth.

But today I'm dying, and I want to say to you what I've never been able to convey:

Shine as only you can, continue lighting up the world with your essence. Laugh without the joy I took away, live without the sorrow I imposed, cry with the nostalgia I bestowed, as the song goes. You are mighty, free, powerful. That's always how I saw you. I'm sorry if I didn't say it enough.

You are everything I ever dreamed of. Now dream yourself and chase those dreams. Keep helping the little creatures, feeding the hummingbirds, and nurturing plants. I trust that you'll know how to take care of yourself. You've already learned.

As I face the end, I recall the time I dozed off while you were getting ready for our wedding in India. When I opened my eyes, I saw the most beautiful woman in the world, adorned in your red sari and glittering jewellery. I've treasured in my heart and carried that image in my mind. I said nothing because I was speechless. I've always been more about action than words. I showed my love as I always told you: 'Actions speak love'. I wish I had known how to say it better. I'm sorry.

It's time for me to go, and I set you free. Thank you for the beauty, for our children, and for everything you gave me.

Goodbye my love,

L.

This letter shows how much L is haunted by the fear of losing his wife. The marriage itself was built on the profound insecurity of two people who kept one another at bay, each promising everything, wanting more and then complaining about not receiving what they felt they had 'paid for'. Secretly, both of them feared that the other might find out they were not good enough and would abandon them. Rather than two pillars of strength, they were like two thin poles on marshy ground leaning on one another, ready to collapse but never quite reaching breaking point, held together as they are by strings and chewing gum. The intensity of their arguments (based on a combination of fear and hope) fuelled their passion and the relationship.

Upon reading this letter, consider why he puts up with her if he believes what he wrote. The truth is he doesn't! Hope drives him. He depicts the masochistic impulse to return to the source of pain, again and again, each time hoping something will give. Of course, part of him knows it won't, but at least the *status quo* is maintained, and he is safe — for the moment. Her victimisation only fuels his hope for a future he is not sure he can handle.

When he writes, 'Gratitude from you scared me', he reveals, for the first time, his vulnerability and unbearable hunger for affection and belonging. But he ends on the same note as at the beginning, asking for forgiveness, blaming himself, and reiterating clearly again, 'I'm sorry!'

The truth is that neither of these people is really seen. At least not yet. After titanic masculine-style reluctance, replete with yells, pounding fists, and threats, the later versions of this letter went through much catharsis before finally arriving at his experiences at a tender age where he, assisted by the consciousness of his Presence, could begin to love himself rather than demand or hope for love from the outside. It is especially difficult for a man to face up to the depths of his feelings, but this one did it beautifully! As always happens, changes in one showed up in the other. She, too, went through a tremendous evolution and waited for him with open arms on the other side of their former life.

COMPLETE LETTERS

The following are examples of letters considered to be complete. They are written to a father, a mother, a best friend, and an attacker.

Letter from a daughter to her father

Hi Daddy,

I've missed you since you left. For so many years before, you were my rock. I remember very well how afraid I was, as a child, to lose you. I never expected it to be like this. I always felt that we had a lot in common: temperament, sensitivity, longing for something more (spirituality). Now that I'm trying to understand your life, I can only see the images.

You were my beloved Daddy — a joyful, hard-working, aboveboard, impulsive, handsome, athletic, resourceful daddy. You taught me how to ride a bike, ski, swim better than anyone else, set up the tent and start a fire. You were a gardener by vocation, a loyal friend, and an honest worker. I saw you keep your word and how you have been helpful to others. I adored you because of that. You were never shy of laughing, fooling around, and having fun. You sometimes overdid it with alcohol; I guess that was what you were fighting about with Mom mostly, but compared to other adults I've known you were able to set the limit.

Thanks to you, in our house there were clear rules, there were consequences, and penalties were meted out. Sometimes too-harsh punishments. They made me weak and terrified, especially naked butt spanks. It was just cruel and that was unnecessary. I was a very sensitive child. The worst was the cold punishments.

You were the bad policeman, and I was a terrified little girl trying to live up to your expectations. When I was little, my great love for you was mixed with fear. I hated you sometimes, but you were so important to me. Why did you get angry so easily? You were an adult,

As always happens, changes in one showed up in the other. She, too, went through a tremendous evolution and waited for him with open arms on the other side of their former life.

after all. Why did you beat me? I was so tiny. Now that I'm a parent myself, I've never felt the need to hit my children. Why did you leave us? Us all? How great and terrible your suffering and fear must have been. I'm so sorry I couldn't help you.

I don't want to remember your presence in my life through the prism of how it ended. I still remember your smell and your fine taste in music and fashion. You were a dad I could be proud of: loving, giving a sense of security, liked and respected by others. You could do so much and fix things; our garden flourished under your care. You know, I dream about it all these years, that you are still there. But memories fade over the years: the sound of your laughter, the taste of your hot radish casserole, warm rolls with honey and milk brought by you from the store in the morning. I loved our camping trips and hiking together. I love them to this day, thanks to you and Mommy.

We lived in difficult times; I felt your fear for the future clearly and inherited this scarcity mindset from you. My pocket money was not enough for basic needs; you gave out money so sparingly. Our most terrible quarrel was about this. You slapped me in the face for lying because I bought face tonic for my acne with the rest of the money from buying shoes. I literally peed myself in fear then. It was scary, but we both knew that if you did that again I'd run away from home.

You yourself have taught me to set boundaries, and you have crossed them yourself. Mommy probably was also scared of you then and every time you got mad. She has never stood up for me, so I guess she agreed with your methods. But you were a great father anyway. I loved you with all my heart and I fell to pieces when you were gone. I'm so sorry you didn't meet your grandchildren, especially my son. You would be a great grandfather.

Your suicide was the scariest thing that ever happened in my life, the most incomprehensible and, therefore, the most terrifying. You were so afraid of madness and that people would say that you were crazy. I know it was your decision, terrifying and excruciatingly painful for us. When Adam called me, saying that you killed yourself, I screamed so loud that the neighbours came to see what had happened. I don't remember what happened to me then. I was in such a shock of pain and despair that I don't remember how I got to our city and home. We loved you so much and we missed you so much the following years. It affected the whole family; your sisters fell into depression. The worst part was that some people condemned you for what you did. My aunts thought it was a sin. We felt that your suffering must have been unbearable. You wouldn't have done it otherwise. Daddy...

I've been worried about your soul for so many years that you might be stuck somewhere in your 'Bardo' of pain and despair. I was sending you love and light while trying to put my life together again without you. I have missed physical help so many times; we had to deal with everything ourselves with Mom and Adam.

It's a pity you never saw my house and garden. I became a gardener just like you. I suddenly found it in my blood. There were so many things I wanted to show and share with you. I am very grateful to you that, thanks to you, I chose men very carefully, even though none could match you in diligence and skills. But I found someone with whom I feel safe and who can make me laugh. You've never met, but you'd probably like each other. He is a good father, just like you.

Daddy, I know you loved me; you were able to give me a sense of a special bond by calling me 'the older, only child'. I know you did your best, taking care of us, in so many ways. I know that you were proud of me. I will never forget your tears of emotion when I got into one of the best universities. I don't know if it's possible, but somehow, you were my Guardian Angel; I felt your help and presence. Thank you for everything, for every difficult and beautiful moment that made me who I am today. Even your death was a kind of gift. It taught me not to take mental pain lightly (and it helps in my work). It gave me the freedom to make my own decisions.

I love you very much,

T.

This farewell required several rewrites before it was accepted by the 'family' group that processed it. The process involved stages of bewilderment, confusion, anger, blame, childhood fears, longing, and finally understanding at the level of the Intelligence of the heart. These experiences were incorporated into a letter that is both a lengthy tribute to her love and a summary of her experiences, now lifted into the graceful acceptance of a seeker of Truth.

——

The process involved stages of bewilderment, confusion, anger, blame, childhood fears, longing, and finally, understanding at the level of the Intelligence of the heart.

——

Today, the student is a noteworthy psychotherapist in her own country, helping many people face their suffering and turn it into a valuable asset in dealing with their lives. This is possible because of her patient and conscious embrace of pain and the life lessons learned in adversity and darkness.

Letter from a daughter to a mother

Dear Mom,

I am dying very soon, and this is my heartfelt goodbye. Thank you so much. Truly, I thank you with all my heart.

I feel that you uplifted each of us. You taught me and my brother and even Dad to always look for the positive and to be thankful for the gift of life, even with all its twists, turns, and unexpected challenges. Even though your way was often heavy, invasive, and dramatic — I see how your hugeness of love, strength of spirit, and sheer physical-emotional perseverance helped forge each of us toward choosing the more noble aspects of ourselves. I loved that you would often say that people will behave in all sorts of troublesome ways, but that we have the choice to respond with integrity and goodwill. You taught us to have compassion and to forgive. I see that tremendous gift from you.

Thank you for the freedoms I expressed as a child. I loved climbing trees, playing with toys mostly meant for boys — like Voltron and Thundercats — many hours of freedom in the woods, and countless times pretending to be a pop star! I felt life coursing through me when I was exuberant, loud, goofy, and tomboyish.

There were some key things you did that hurt me, my brother, and dad.

I see the ways that you blocked and suppressed my energies during my childhood — and I see how I continued those patterns through adulthood. Of course, most parents want to encourage harmonious behaviour in their child, but all the rules of your religion and all the ways of how you thought things should be — I felt like I couldn't be fully human around you; I didn't feel safe to embody anything related to sensuality or to ask you anything about sexuality, and situations and relationships that didn't fit your norms were considered taboo and for people who were somehow lesser. This all contributed to my lack of contact with my whole self.

You valued 'doing' disproportionately more than 'being'. But that highlighted for me the importance of beingness, which I later practised regularly in my life. And I see that your doingness was your trying to make a difference in the business world, which was so dominated by male power, and at the same time, you were doing everything you could to serve our family and run the household.

Your compulsion for constant verbalising left little space for observing or being deeply present. I copied this behaviour in childhood and young adulthood; I was often bossy and impenetrable. It was uncomfortable, yet I am grateful for those experiences because they taught me the necessity to shed the armour and to feel a fuller spectrum by being more porous and more open to people and life in all its forms.

As a child, when I began to perceive many rules from you about what's right and wrong, and I didn't see much room for grey area, I began to hide some things from you out of necessity. I began to associate naturalness, sensuality, sexuality, frankness, and even just some things that are humorous, with a sense of heaviness and wrongness. I see that I maintained that cutting-apart of myself, long past when it was necessary. But I came to see that the rigidity you adhered to was partly due to your own upbringing and your being the middle child of five kids. And your religion gave you structure amidst the chaos of life. When we swing towards the extremes, we can later see and feel where the middle point is. I thank you, because although it took some time, I really do know where my healthy middle ground is. And I can now say that I later owned my creation of not having a more open and expressed relationship with myself. I see that many of the limitations I initially absorbed from you were exactly what I needed to work on and liberate in myself.

Beyond any pains and challenges that we brought to each other, our love for each other is absolutely greater. I admire your power and I feel your love. Your power was great enough to manifest the home, clothes, food, and so much more of what each of us needed and wanted. Your actions, and simply what you radiate, made the whole nuclear and extended family feel loved and appreciated. All the holiday celebrations, family reunions, your happily hosting my sleepovers and parties, your sending endless greeting cards and letters to family, loved ones, and neighbours. Thanks to you, I experienced the love that comes from writing thank-you cards to people :)

I admire your tenacity, your work ethic, your superhuman ability to sleep so few hours per night, to work as a top executive in corporations and non-profits… to help put Dad through university first and then you went to university and you graduated summa cum laude with a triple major — while working a full-time job, with two children at home, and you were a member, often a leader, of several boards and committees. And still I remember countless evenings of delicious home-cooked meals and you asking me daily what I experienced at school and extracurricular activities. You always encouraged us to talk about our days.

On a bigger note, you helped Dad heal from alcoholism… That was quite miraculous. What impacted me so much was that, even though your initial reaction to many difficult situations was staunch resistance, you always eventually opened into huge-hearted acceptance of what was. And you became much faster at that over the years! As I write this letter, the biggest feeling that pervades is that I celebrate you!

Seeing the wholeness in you, and the wholeness in me, is how I can truly say goodbye. I am grateful. This is genuinely a good goodbye. I love you.

C.

> Seeing the wholeness in you, and the wholeness in me, is how I can truly say goodbye.

The need to say not-so-nice things the way they were perceived and not the way we later, naturally, re-interpret them is of utmost importance.

She really nailed it. The letter culminated a long process of examination, justification, excusing herself and her mother, failing to take space for herself, and finally admitting just how much her mother had taught her that strengthened her as a woman in today's world. I think that many women can identify with this letter, whether they are a daughter or an active business mum, a mother one could be measured against! Especially in the USA.

Letter to a best friend

My dear Kathryn,

We have shared so much of 'life' together, even in the relatively short 16 years we have known each other as best friends. These have been the years that shaped so much of who we are and who we became in this life.

With the myriad memories that captivate me, I find writing this letter to you before my death particularly hard. How can I truly say goodbye and let go of someone I love so dearly... As you know, I really hate goodbyes.

I often try to recall what precisely drew me to you with such intensity from our first meeting. It may have just been two professional women slugging away at being 'just' young mothers and the simple enjoyment of laughing together... so many fun travels and nights out and so much joy. But such a true and uncommon love grew in any case.

The hard bits of life quite quickly reared their head. It was a privilege to be your support through your husband's affair and eventual divorce. I know I have often joked that I have been through two divorces, as supporting you through yours was so personal to me too. I often felt more indignant towards James than you did.

When your mother was diagnosed with cancer at the same time, I couldn't fathom how you must have felt, and again, I just wanted to shield you from any more pain. Your mother eventually passed away, and I felt your pain acutely. I delighted in being 'the one' you would turn to in those times and relished being able to bring you some lightness despite how much pain you were in.

Even those years of hard times are recalled with joy. Those moments of searching for our path in life and surviving took us on great adventures, and all I remember from them was the laughter — even through the tears. We always found a reason to laugh...

While you were on the single scene again, kissing frogs and dreaming of finding love, I began my own divorce. We were always so struck by how similar our paths in life have been.

My mother was also diagnosed with terminal cancer, and my divorce was nearly killing me. This was when you met Paul. No one could have been more thrilled at your finding love again than me.

I recall those sequences of events with an almost photographic memory because of how much pain they caused me eventually.

While you were in the throes of new love, I was in utter misery. I wanted us to be like we had always been — talking daily and being each other's 'first choice'. I wanted no one but you to comfort me and just be there for me. I also was too proud to ask you for that, quietly judging you for not being better. And the pain this caused me consumed me.

I felt so confused as to how, despite having been through nearly the exact same experience, it seemed you couldn't find time for me. I felt abandoned. I remember that time so clearly, wondering 'Why do I ALSO have to lose my best friend amidst the devastating loss of my mother and my marriage?' And, 'How could she of all people not care enough to just be there for me?' I was so completely crushed.

Sadness was replaced by anger — intense anger — which eventually gave way to righteousness, and only with hindsight can I see how harshly I judged you. The very notion of how similar our situations were but how differently we treated each other through them and how I interpreted that as such violent injustice became such a consuming narrative for me. I could not let go of how ALONE you 'made' me feel. I blamed you for making all of my pain even worse.

With Paul, and all his wealth, you were also given opportunities and privileges that most people could only dream of — all at a time when my own financial landscape looked so scary. I watched you change with all this money, adjusting to the power it brought to you. I remember when you tried to give me your air miles, as you 'would never have to pay for airline tickets again', but then you wanted to dictate how I could use them. I was so mortally offended and utterly indignant when I tried to use them for a flight to Kenya after my mother had died, and you told me that that's not what the miles were intended for with such an air of superiority.

'Assert yourself above everyone else, but do not dare do that to me', I recall righteously exclaiming with a huge pride inside my head. I returned all the miles to you with such indignant pride, convinced that you were no longer the person I had cared for so deeply.

I listened to people tell me how 'money changes people', and I needed to let go of you. You ran in different circles now and were so enamoured by the glamour.

Life then dealt me one more blow that it had spared you. My father died without warning. You knew he was my hero — my idealised idol — and that his death would be the hardest thing in my life... but, yet again, you were nowhere to be found.

For me, it was the final straw. I was prepared to give you up and accept that 'people change with money' and that you were a seasonal — not a lifetime — friend. I got to put myself in the place of the victim and then, with righteousness, judge you for changing and not being a good enough friend (by my standards).

But what I can only see now is that I could only ever see my own perspective. I couldn't see that my demands on you for behaving in a way that was 'not good enough' were the limitations that my judgmental nature had created. I simply couldn't entertain another perspective.

I can see now that my declared love came with so many conditions. All my ideals for a 'very best friend' were of my own making. My comparing how I behaved versus how you behaved in similar scenarios was used to make me better and you worse. I did all this under the guise of love and friendship... but only now can I see that this is not friendship or true love at all. This was loving with conditions and demands.

All the good fortunes that came to you after your divorce were the same things I always wanted too, which I suspect made it even harder for me. I know in my deepest heart; I didn't want you not to not have them... but I know I really wanted what you had. Paul came along and embraced your children as if they were his own — and I craved nothing more than this notion of family that I had spent a lifetime idealising.

But I can only see now that my notions of 'family' are constructs of my own making and thus illusions that seem to disappear like vapour behind expectations and demands that are simply not real. I see now that the souls we choose to have in our life make up our 'family'. This has been a hard thing for me to accept in this lifetime, and I can see how you were such a big part of teaching me this. What this taught me most was that no one can give me the love I craved so desperately from you besides myself.

I can see now that we come into existence alone and alone we will go... Demanding that you 'be there' for me was a reflection of my own dependency. I struggled so much to accept the change when everything around me was changing so much. I couldn't stop for even a moment to consider how you must have felt in it all. Of course, we did make it back to each other as we both began to learn about ourselves.

I can only now see so clearly how my idealisations and notions of how relationships 'should be' were contributing to the strain between us. Now when I look at you and our 'story', I feel nothing but complete compassion and immense gratitude. I can see that being able to stand on my own two feet and letting go of my judgments of how things 'ought to be' have freed me in a way I didn't know I needed. Thank you.

Because I am at the end of this life, I wish you to know how knowing you and growing in myself has been the greatest lesson of this lifetime. You have taught me what love is — true and unconditional love — and that has made my life worthwhile.

I have always delighted so much in being with you, and even recalling our laughter gives me a smile now as I write these final words.

I will forever be grateful.

With my entire heart,

Josephine

It reminded me that friendship is the highest expression of earthly love.

This letter says it all. It is complete and clear. The only thing that cannot be conveyed here in text form is the atmosphere in which it was read between two dear friends. It was deeply emotional and moving without being 'mushy' or sentimental, expressing a liberation and a truth-telling experience that was only revealed then and there. It reminded me that friendship is the highest expression of earthly love.

Letter to an attacker

To my attacker,

As I sit here and reflect on writing a goodbye letter to you at the end of my life, it occurs to me that whilst I have a clear image of you in my mind's eye, I do not know your name. I do now know what to call you.

And yet, you have played a major part in the crafting of the last 19 years of my life. We did not meet in a way that is 'normal', and you certainly were not like any taxi driver giving me a ride home. The judge told me in court that, despite believing me, there was not enough evidence to prosecute, as I had been drinking. My fault, the Victim.

I never suspected that you would be the person to show me what it means to forgive unconditionally, to feel what it means to deeply surrender, or to be the one that helped me see what it means to truly stand in my own Power.

This has not always been the case, and the feelings of Victimhood have been so deeply ingrained in my being that they have often burst out in anger and despair at life's vicissitudes.

When you raped me in my own home, my first home of my own, I revelled in the pain and the drama. I felt broken inside, and it was perfect, the tarnished broken part felt that this was what I deserved; I chose you to help me symbolise this pain and feeling of being broken. I gave you the power over me; everything you symbolised made me powerless. The desire to be seen, to be noticed, was all part of the same story; I created it and made it about you. I made you the significant holder of my pain, not always so obviously, but I had internalised it to such a degree that it was ingrained in my being, alienating me from life.

It has been all so encompassing, and I now give this all back to you. The word *rape* is so clear in its explanation and associated with an abuse of power. I have reclaimed this as my own Power. Not yours.

I was already on a path of self-discovery, and, thanks to you, I deep-dove into that and have found ultimate strength and freedom in Self. In the deep knowing within my being that I AM that I AM — that I created this life in my formative years to give me the curiosity and fervent desire to be of service to others. In my knowingness of Self, I am able to know others and understand that the ultimate Love and Forgiveness in life comes from soul embodiment.

What I have for myself is the strength and the power to know that what I have created in you I can now create for myself, and the ultimate power of forgiveness is the strength I feel and the deep gratitude to live my life.

——

I never suspected that you would be the person to show me what it means to forgive unconditionally, to feel what it means to deeply surrender, or to be the one that helped me see what it means to truly stand in my own Power.

——

Without this experience, I do not believe that I would have found the strength to rise into the fulness of myself, and the wisdom and knowledge to understand that being in Service to Humanity is unselfish Joy and Freedom in this lifetime. For this, I thank you.

S.

It is interesting how this letter winds to its conclusion. This is a strong letter that shocks while striking a chord that resonates deeply, in an unusual way, just like the awakening of its writer — a passionate, vibrant, dramatic woman who has tasted life in full and in depth.

Emotion is the key to transmutation.

The role of listener confers enormous responsibility and authority. You must tune into the person's heart to help them unburden themselves and reach the state of awareness of forgiveness and recognition of their life lesson. As a member of a group, you will be the voice of their conscience, helping them directly or indirectly to move beyond confusion to clarity.

This process is not about self-indulgence or exaggeration. No one will applaud the victim or condemn the aggressor. It is about the release of energies to be redirected and raised, without which no emancipation is possible. For example, when you want to cry, you create the habit of swallowing your words and constricting the larynx and vocal cords while the jaw becomes rigid — yet maybe what you truly want to do is roar with fury! Whether it's ourselves, or the other person: stop, feel, and express safely for your own health's sake.

Apart from the guidelines received to correct expression, a letter should be read in its entirety without interruptions. As a listener, you take note not only of how it is read and the tone of voice but also of what words it uses, what it says, how it says it, and finally, what it does *not* say. Once the reading is complete, the support person or group should give a response to the letter and then there should be a response from the writer. This constructive criticism should be as clear and direct as possible, always accompanied by a specific example and a suggestion of how it could be said better — one that uplifts and inspires the reader. When it comes to what is 'missing' you will rely on your common sense: what you

> This process is not about self-indulgence or exaggeration. No one will applaud the victim or condemn the aggressor. It is about the release of energies to be redirected and raised.

feel, what doesn't quite 'smell' right or authentic to you. You should be direct and sincere, just as you would want a listener to be with you.

You may already realise that the role of listener is continually working on you, demanding from you what you would not dare in ordinary life: to be yourself and speak up. Most people dislike giving criticism, no matter how constructive, whether for fear of standing out, provoking the other person's anger or rejection, creating dependency, or losing their role as 'poor little me who needs protection'. But, in this work, everyone must show up and assume a position — it's part of the process.

The first reading of a letter is completed when your group or support person has given their opinion and the reader has noted the suggested changes. That is the general goal, but you must establish your own system.

When writing your own letters, I recommend that you start with the easiest ones, but if you sense that the real problem is elsewhere and the current letter is going nowhere, you could address another relationship first. Many begin with the parents, but these are often the most difficult letters because the subject cannot be seen directly. It may take another relationship to reveal the former. This is called *projection*: the transfer of desired or feared qualities onto another. All too often, people marry their mother or their father in an attempt to change them symbolically or obtain what they never received.

This exercise will help you discover the humanity that resides in you and the unconditional support of that Source to which you have direct access. By loving the other, you learn to love yourself; by loving yourself, you will love the other. And, in the process, you will discover the purest and most selfless love, Friendship.

LETTERS TO SELF AND TO PRESENCE

In our School, after processing the letters in small 'family' groups, we undertake the letter-burning ritual outlined below. But before setting fire to everything they have written, each student will have spent time alone the previous evening in a state of alignment[8] to write two more letters: a farewell letter from the personality-self to their Presence and one from their Presence to the self. This is a time of deep understanding and

---

8 As per the Master Practice presented in pp. 7-11.

> By loving the other, you learn to love yourself; by loving yourself, you will love the other. And, in the process, you will discover the purest and most selfless love, Friendship.

revelation about the life they have led and who and what they truly are. It is a time for communion with the soul.

The following letters from former students serve as examples of this process. Once everything is said and done, the students also write their epitaph. These letters and their epitaphs are the only pieces of writing not to be consumed by fire.

Letters from Presence to Personality-self

Sweet girl. Sweet child of the Light.

I watched you play. Watched you search. Watched you tumble. Watched you fall. Watched you love. Watched you try so hard.

I saw how lost you were.

Saw you fumbling in the dark. Saw you sleepwalking, searching blindfolded.

Saw you start to remove the blindfold in awe.

Saw your heart. Saw your dedication.

Saw your pain in the knowledge that you'd harmed others.

Saw your big, big human heart. Saw you wanting to be more for others.

Saw your version of service.

Saw you wanting to save the world without truly knowing how to save yourself.

Saw your raw determination, your will, your desire for that which is perfect.

Sweet girl. You did so well. You did so very well.

You didn't fail. Do you hear me singing that in your ear and resonating that in your heart?

Listen again to me, sweet, sweet girl, you did not fail. You did it all beautifully.

Now be at peace and know that I never abandoned you and always loved you just the way you were.

Truly.

Listen again to me, sweet, sweet girl, you did not fail. You did it all beautifully.

Dearest Personality-self,

It is I, you, I AM and all that is.

I wanted to express my deepest love for you on the eve of my next voyage into the unknown.

I have watched over you, from within, and loved you from the day you were born.

Always seeing, sensing, feeling, and guiding.

I have watched you go beyond the limitations of fear, letting go of your ego and embracing the truth inside of you, which is fearless.

I have watched you observe yourself, with judgement and without.

I have watched you transform your fear into love.

I have watched you experience pain and inflict it upon others, disconnected from your true Source.

I have watched you see a stranger through the eyes of compassion and realise that the stranger is you.

I have watched you learn to give the nourishment of light.

I have watched your intention create your reality.

I have watched you step away from the judge's chair and see the gulf of separation between 'right' and 'wrong'.

I have watched the turbulence in your mind interfere with the creativity of your soul.

I have watched your willingness to expand your heart and contact your connection with all that exists.

I have watched you let go of all expectations and know that Love is the only reality.

I have watched your divine Intelligence be the spark of life force that energises your body.

I have watched you learn the 'act of love' in its truest sense, for yourself and others.

I have watched you return to yourself and set yourself free.

I AM a master of divine expression and you have spoken through me.

I AM LOVE and I am free.

I AM a master of divine expression and you have spoken through me.
I AM LOVE and I am free.

To my Presence, my Creator,

Thank you.

You were always there within me. Everywhere. Guiding me. Loving me.

I searched to understand you first in books and meditation; and in others.

My search for you shaped the very meaning of my life – the perfectionism I strived for. I wanted to embody you to the fullest.

It was the greatest love game of hide and seek and I am so grateful for the journey, for it all.

You were my inspiration and are my True Love.

You were always there. In my heart, in the air, in the song of the birds, in the smell of the earth, in the vastness of the sky; everywhere and nowhere, everything and nothing and always present within me, Love.

I tried so hard to understand you and to help others understand you too.

I dedicated the end of my life to feeling you within my heart and body and trying to help others know and feel you also.

I depart this world with so much gratitude and with the knowing that I am ever and forever your humblest servant.

Thank you for my life, my body and for all those who touched me and whom I also touched. Thank you for everything.

Thank you, thank you, thank you.

Dear Presence,

In the language of my heart, I want to tell you that I know you and feel you are here, as you have always been, from within.

I want to express my deepest gratitude to you for releasing me from the notion of separation — separation from my truest form and essence and separation from all of creation.

I now know the truest meaning of the word 'trust' and realise that it is only when listening to the voice of my own Spirit that I can connect with Truth and be truthful with others.

You have taught me that it is only through surrendering and acceptance that I can fully embrace ALL that I AM. There is no 'lack' or 'fear' — only Love.

I thank you for showing me that I AM limitless, and I AM you in action.

I AM nothing but I AM everything.

I thank you for guiding me through the many difficult life lessons that I have chosen, knowing that they have been invaluable for my spiritual growth.

I thank you for the experience of divine mind, releasing me from the illusion of judgement, shame, and guilt.

I thank you for the full Knowing that I am never alone.

I thank you for the immeasurable joy I feel when I am carefree, living in unity with creation, and feeling the ebb and flow of the darkness and the light.

You are Everything and all that is beyond my perception. You have shown me how to dedicate my life to knowing and understanding my Self and that, only by doing this, can one truly love oneself and others.

I thank you from the depths of my soul for showing me the true path of light, knowing that I am in Service.

I have only ever known Love through you.

With Love and Gratitude and Joy.

 BURNING OF THE LETTERS

Of all the physical elements, fire is the only multidimensional expression of life. It consumes the dross and purifies whatever it burns. Fire also serves as an emissary between planes of life, transporting the refined product into a higher expression. We use it in our process of ego-death to burn the letters at the very end, once all is said and done, and the person has freed themselves and all those related to them.

When you and your group or support person conclude that you expressed your deepest and most vulnerable feelings towards your individual relationships in the letters, I recommend that you meet and perform the following ceremony of burning the farewell letters, preferably in the open air with the help of a pyre.

Of all the physical elements, fire is the only multidimensional expression of life. It consumes the dross and purifies whatever it burns.

If this is not possible, the letters can be burnt symbolically by visualising the violet flame destroying them. Here are two suggested ceremony formats:

OPTION 1

Invoking Elohim (Hebrew for God, Gods, or the Godhead). In this ceremony, the elemental Presences of nature and the Elohim, who are pure Fire Beings, are invoked.

'ELOAHIM' or Elohim are invoked thusly: by chanting Eh-lo-ah-heem (seven times, with the 'h' aspirated as in English).

The Salamanders (the elemental emissions of the Elohim) are then asked to symbolically burn the letters, consuming with them all energetic records of the past. They are also asked to burn all our desires, transmuting them into light.

OPTION 2

The following Buddhist prayer may then be read out loud together:

To the Divine Body of Unknowable, Infinite Truth,
To the Divine Body of Perfect Knowledge,
To the Divine Body of the Voice of Silence,
To the Divine Body of Transcendental Feeling,
To the Divine Body of the Mind of the Cosmos,
To the Divine Body of the Thoughtless Consciousness,
To the Divine Master, the Eternal Guide of the Inner World,
And to the Invisible Guide of the Outer World — the Guide and Protector of all Sentient Life,
To the Divine Teachers, those of the Divine Body of Perfect Knowledge and the Divine Body of Incarnation,
To the Divine Guides of the Subtle World, who gave sacrificially of their time and themselves, to aid those who did not awaken to attain perfection,
To the Divine Lord of Death, the Eternal Guide of the Subtle World, who sacrificed his redemption for the redemption of mankind,
To the Divine Body of the Primordial Being,
To the Divine Body of the Perfect Sacrifice,
We pay homage and prayer,
We offer Love and Hope,
We offer our gratitude.

LIFE LESSONS

A life lesson reveals that aspect of divinity you came to manifest concretely through personal experience, be it private or professional. It is what you came to do. You get a fairly clear picture of this during the revision of your life through your relationships.

Virtues such as compassion, unconditional love, faith, and freedom are not life lessons but rather qualities that enhance the particular task you chose in this lifetime. The difficulties you have faced indicate the lessons learned — for example, how you managed your emotions and resources.

The north node in astrology or numerology readings hints at what that task might be in the long run. In particular, it indicates the energetic qualities you need in order to accomplish your ultimate life task. But before discovering your Life task, you must obviously understand and embrace the individual life lessons that prepare you for it.

Life lessons respond to the needs of your life task. The latter emerges from within, in a posture of maturity, acknowledging whatever is most gratifying and fulfilling.

The farewell letters, especially those concerning difficult relationships, reveal valuable lessons in energy mastery learned through adversity. There are also lessons learned in favourable conditions. This is the right time to review the main ones: those imparted through bloodlines, namely the mother and father. All this occurs within the mindset of the *Alchemical Alignment*, holding the focus of Consciousness from a neutral perspective — that of the Christ Self or brotherly love.

The overall Life Lesson for this embodiment concerns what you can offer and what you can give of yourself in Service. Ultimately, that is how you will find fulfilment.

The current issue of our times involves learning to work with others, ideally in a committed group, as humanity prepares for group consciousness. This will require a well-defined personal identity as an individual free from egoism. In a group, everyone must position themselves equally — as their different strengths combine to form a united collective spirit.

How you grew up, how you built your character, what your parents gave you or did not, these are not life lessons, as such, but tools that enabled you to embrace your life lessons. They reveal the contribution made by your relationship with your parents and others to the entire picture.

Virtues such as compassion, unconditional love, faith, and freedom are not life lessons but rather qualities that enhance the particular task you chose in this lifetime.

The emergence of virtues such as compassion, respect, and consideration for others defines your level of humanity. The heart must break many times. The images you build of yourself are always false. To recognise all of that spells maturity. Experiences of pain and helplessness characteristically mark the spiritual path that eventually leads to transcendence. These are the foundations that ultimately provide access to higher dimensions, enabling you to experience real joy and happiness through humility and brotherhood.

During the process of 'clearing the pathway to becoming', regardless of whether people still lived or had passed on, you wrote farewell letters to those beings who have had the most importance in your life, starting with your father and mother. You reviewed those letters repeatedly until you came to see the experience from a neutral perspective. That greater understanding allowed you to discover yourself and detect what you still need to learn.

—

Experiences of pain and helplessness characteristically mark the spiritual path that eventually leads to transcendence.

—

Proceed now to discover and understand from a higher vantage point the following pointers:

- Describe the climate into which you were born to gain insight into who you are today and what you are best equipped for.
- What difficulties and benefits did your family and conditions present?
- What did your mother bequeath to you or elicit from you? Your father? How have you applied these 'legacies'?
- Consider the absence of certain experiences and how their lack also shaped you.
- Also, review your experiences to notice what you attracted and to understand why. Just concentrate on whatever it was they led you to learn. Then extricate from those lessons the best part, the positive qualities you now possess.
- What situations constantly repeat themselves for you? What does life seem to be asking of you? What is easy and what remains difficult?
- Now review all the lessons life has offered you from a global perspective. Is there a common denominator?
- Finally, in your posture of the *Alchemical Alignment*, look at these life lessons and your personality-self from the higher perspective of the soul. From there, choose the most valuable and find the similarities.
- What is your soul revealing to you at this moment?

- Equally, review your faculties and talents. Assess how you have used them. What better use could you make of them?
- Before concluding, take one more step towards self-discovery and revelation.

When you are satisfied that you have completed the farewell letters and life-lessons stages to your fullest ability, you are then ready to embark on the meditation process of ego-death in Part Four.

PART FOUR

THE PROCESS OF EGO-DEATH

The following process can give you insight into the ritualistic frame surrounding the ancient and complex science of dying. It traces the effect of dissolving energy forms within the human psyche, the varied motion of Mind — unwinding and then reformulating — and the workings of Consciousness as it seeks fusion with Spirit and the regeneration of human life.

The Death of the Ego

Please note that this process was meant to be used in conjunction with extensive individual preparation over a full year at the levels performed in our School of Consciousness. This would include a detailed study of the Buddhist Wheel of Karma (discussed in Part Five) and its automatic reflex sequence and transcendental possibilities. At our School, we teach the art of subtle perception, self-re-creation, and energy management of Light and force.

To help avoid harm or undue shock, the personality and Spirit are meticulously evoked and processed as part of the overall preparation. This is very different to what occurs spontaneously in natural death, where the individual lacks information about what lies ahead and may be unable to face or control emotions that lead to fear, panic, or sudden unwarranted embodiment in lower life forms.

In some extraordinary situations, this text alone might help educate a dying person, in which case a subsequent reading of it would be useful when their time comes. While doing so, they should allow for parallel images and deep insight into their own dynamics to uncover the truth contained in the ancient teachings here and adapted to modern times.

Before moving on to this meditation, sit or lie still and follow the Master Practice meditation (the *Alchemical Alignment*), at the beginning of this book (pp. 8-11). This enables you to access Spirit-life in the highest dimension.

The entire process of the ego-death meditation usually lasts from two to three hours in complete darkness with music that changes to induce the desired mood. The participant lies down, usually blindfolded with the body comfortable.

Deep breathing induces relaxation and accelerates the Light body (Points of Light within the cells) to release itself from matter temporarily. The tone is intimate and always slow, clear, and deep, evoking ritual recitation, prayer, and incantation. There are long pauses included for the assimilation of visualisation and experience.

You can choose whether to record the following meditation in your own voice or listen to my voice in the audiobook of this text.[9] If reading it yourself, you can achieve the most intimate and effective result by using a slow, rhythmic, but emphatic tone throughout. This is the best way to hold the attention.

> To help avoid harm or undue shock, the personality and Spirit are meticulously evoked and processed as part of the overall preparation.

---

9 The audiobook can be found on the website of our School (www.zrsoc.com) or in LightEn's Library of Light (www.light-en.org).

The following statement may be affirmed in the singular, or it may be changed to the plural for all humanity. In either case, it must be uttered sincerely.

 PREPARATION MEDITATION

STAGE ONE

Declaration by the Traveller

I have reviewed my life, and I find it satisfactory.
I have corrected the errors of the past, according to my best understanding.
I have understood and learned the lessons offered in Love and in suffering, according to my ability.
I have asked for forgiveness, and I have accepted the fact that I have been forgiven.
I have discovered and honoured my Real Centre — the Essence 'I AM'.
I have embraced my own imperfections and those of others.
I have learned to Love.
I have understood that I still have more to learn.
I look to the future with determined courage, faith, and trust.
I accept the verdict of God the Almighty, which is my own Consciousness.
I ask to be prepared for a conscious life in service of the All, which is myself, as All is in me, and I myself am in All.

STAGE TWO

Let us pray.

Asatho Maa Sad Gamaya	(Lead me… from the unreal to the real.)
Thamaso Maa Jyothir Gamaya	(Lead me… from darkness to Light.)
Mrithyor Maa Amritham Gamaya	(Lead me… from death to immortality.)
Om, shanti, shanti, shanti	(Om, peace, peace, peace.)

Bliss to the whole Universe.
Peace to the whole Universe.
Abundance to the whole Universe.
Supreme Goodness for all Beings in the Universe.
Peace, Peace, Peace to the whole Universe.
Om, Shanti, Shanti, Shanti.

STAGE THREE

You now understand the process of death.

You know that ego-dying is the same as physical death.

The same pain, the same surrender, the same helplessness that you are now prepared to experience.

Remember that in ego-dying now, your body remains poised upon the earth, held and protected by it.

It is not involved.

Draw your Tube of Light around your body and see it encircled by the grace and love of your Divine Presence.

You are prepared to relinquish your old identity, and the useless reflexes that have tied you to unconscious patterns that lead nowhere safe or healthy. You are ready to meet your Real Self at the highest levels of intimacy and transparency.

You are ready for Revelation.

You have forgiven and felt forgiven.

You have severed your attachments and dissolved your antipathies.

You have learned to contain your impulses in the light of your greater desire for peace and well-being.

All this you have done in preparation for this, the greatest Journey of existence.

You have learned to align, and in this posture… you have reached awareness of your true reality and have sensed the fullness of inner light as your Spirit Self.

You have made the distinction between the subjective voice of your comfortable habits and the still, small voice of your soul… that speaks to you through yearnings and promises a joy that is everlasting because it reveals your own nature.

You are whole and perfect, and you are prepared to live it.

This is why you wish to leave your little self behind and touch upon a timeless, spaceless dimension… with no reference points.

You can now embrace the Nothingness… which for your innermost Self is Everything-ness, the All.

So relax now, fully, releasing the control of your mind over the body.

Align yourself between the heavens and the earth, visualising your connection as a flow of light between the poles above and below.

Your connection to the earth below is strong.

It is a magnetism capable of sustaining and nourishing you, even when you withdraw your awareness of it. This part of you will feel safe and sustained.

Now… Take a last look at the planet that has been your home and all the places you have loved.

Float past the beautiful greenery, the luscious flora, and the vibrant fauna that share this earth with you.

Take a last look at your loved ones and again bless and thank each one.

Pause

Resist any temptation, any feeling of attraction, repulsion, or curiosity pertaining to your former life.

Centre in your heart and allow it to be filled with the warmth of your innermost yearnings.

Trust in that Presence and that inner voice. Trust your Self.

Allow the electronic force of your Divine Presence in the Alchemical Alignment, to draw you upwards and deposit you in the arms of the divine as if it were the breast of the Beloved, without fear or longings, knowing you have lived your life up to now as best you could.

You are empty of the self that you have been but full of that inner satisfaction, the glory and intimacy of the light beyond.

Pause

Truth is Absolute.

Allow your mind to unravel while your attention remains in the heart, in the acknowledgement of eternal joy that is your Real nature.

As you die to the old, the new will emerge, evoked by the dictates of your soul.

IT knows! As you Know… that you Know… even if your little mind does not yet understand.

Remember: You are Whole.

As you leave the past behind, you leave behind all that coarsened or made you insensitive.

You become extremely receptive to vibrations, especially the emotions.

Stay firm in the trust of your heart.

Surrender to it, as you prepare for the greatest moment of your life.

During the dying process, when your past actions come up for review, lying or avoiding is impossible.

Instead, understand, forgive, and accept yourself.

In that acceptance lies impeccability and integrity.

Acceptance is the power of life and its transmuting fire.

This alchemy of transmutation is the key to eternal life.

You need not make an effort to awaken: When you stop acting and reacting… when there is no longer a struggle to be this or that…

You will find yourself awake.

Pause

Dying unveils the great formula for manifestation: the deliberate and conscious management of energy and force.

When the time comes to return to the Earth plane, that will be the moment for regeneration and accumulation of momentum.

Hold your thoughts. Hold your feelings in the stillness of the eternal present. Be in the Silence and feel its texture, the pressure of the Pure Mind that is your Essence as it seeks to create in Perfection.

Visualise and energise the life you wish to lead… You are one with the Source of all manifestation; power and control are within you.

Pause

You have the right to choose your life.

Choose Truth, choose Beauty, choose Harmony…

Know that you are Light, source of love and wisdom, and that your real Self never dies.

Knowing without knowledge, you understand the totality of your existence.

When the time comes, you will feel the energy of life entering into the atoms of the physical body, re-creating itself in Light.

You will feel the peace, the new life, the harmony, the holiness of the matter of your body, the translucent substance of your mind and of your emotions.

You will breathe the fullness of a new life into your body and world.

And feel the glory of rebirth as the seedling of God awakened in you.

Pause

You are guided, protected, illumined and sustained by the Light.
You are an expression of the Infinite.
Unrepeatable.
Unique.
And Perfect.
Now… discover your Eternal Self.

STAGE FOUR

The moment of surrender has arrived.

A part of your Consciousness will remain with your physical body, and another will follow the process that will bring you closer to the purity of your original essence.

Link yourself now with your Inner Master: this is the 'I AM' Presence or Spirit-Self.

Feel protected and loved. Your experience now is exclusively vibrational. There is nothing to understand.

Relax the physical body. Breathe fully and deeply and let go on the exhalation as if you were going into a long sleep after a day full of activity that has left you tired.

Relax your mind… releasing the control it holds over the body. Withdraw the attention from the muscles and address yourself to the inside of your body.

Direct your attention towards the centre of the heart and reaffirm your essential longing: Peace, Light, and Harmony.

Feel the heart as a radiant, serene, joyful, and simultaneously expectant state of Being.

Peace, Light, and Harmony…

Sense how your body is composed of thousands of millions of scintillating particles of Light.

Become aware of the weight of physical matter and, at the same time, of the electrical lightness of the Points of Light at the centre of each cell.

The Points of Light respond to the Central Sun in your heart. The more you feel and generate, the greater the Light expands. The greater the Sun in your breast, the greater the Light in all parts of your body.

Now feel the pulsation of the earth under your body exerting a magnetic attraction similar to the pulsation in your own heart. Surrender your body to the protection of Mother Earth.

Similarly, feel the particles of Light intensifying as they become an electrical wave that sweeps over the whole body — light with matter, intensifying and reverberating in greater and greater waves, extending below the feet and alternating in waves upwards towards the head.

Take your time.

Huge waves of electrical impulse oscillate from below upwards...

From above downwards...

Sweeping your body of Light as it intensifies its frequency and feels like it wants to separate from the physical...

Meanwhile, your physical body rests very deeply.

Consciousness begins to release itself from the physical body — vacillating, balancing itself tenuously like an electrical tremor above the body.

You feel a strong impulse to reach upwards...

At one point, you reach a peak where a powerful explosion of Light, like a centrifugal spiral, emerges within the Tube of Light propelling you higher and higher...

Surrender to this force stemming from the heart, combined with the vibrant force of the third eye, awakening a tremendous energy in your body of light.

You hear an effervescent sound within — a white sound, like snow and luminous diamond-like particles...

It is the sound of Silence...

The body remains serene, poised upon the earth, but your Consciousness rises into the Silence.

Identify yourself solely with Consciousness and that effervescent space. Do not become distracted by the sensations or emotions that your body might feel.

Understand: You are Light, the Light of Intelligence that directs forces of life.

You are an integral part of the All. This is your great opportunity to re-create yourself in perfection.

You continue to rise, accelerate... rising and accelerating...

Releasing... whirling... entering a silence beyond the known.

The four great Archangels, guardians of the elements, surround you and protect you.

Journey into a timeless, spaceless dimension with no reference points... Nothingness... the Great Void of the Clear Light.

Identify yourself only with Consciousness and with that space of Light. Trust your Spirit Self...

Enter wholly into that Silence, into that Light, into that field of electricity... within and through the Tube of Light, which resembles a tunnel of Light in the darkness of creation — beyond time, beyond the mind, beyond the known... through a spiral of Light that takes you to the centre of creation!

Confront the Primordial Light: the Light of Creation, without time, without form, without space...

You are Light, Pure Light!

Affirm:

I AM Light.
I AM the source of Love and Wisdom.
Knowing without knowledge, I understand the totality of my existence.

Silence.

 THE PROCESS

PART I
First Flash: I AM
Inconceivable ecstasy; you are One and indivisible...

You are *All-One*, alone but full: whole. All is within you.

You find yourself in a dimension without time or space, without points of reference... in Nothingness... within the Clear Void Light that is Every-thing-ness.

You are an enormous energetic field — like an immense electric ocean, pulsing, dancing, irradiating, exploding, weaving itself continuously...
...within a space where energy becomes form and form returns to subatomic energy.

You are Light without centre, empty and clear. You are the void that contains all possibility. Pure Light…

Second Flash: I AM THAT I AM

You now have a sensation of centricity.

You perceive through a focus — your heart…

You barely have a sense of form; it is more a movement, a flow.

You are a luminous centre of force and power!

Repeat inside yourself:

I AM the Source of Love and Wisdom. Knowing with knowledge,
I understand the totality of my existence.

PART II

The Reality of the Mind — Creating and Animating Thoughtforms and Emotions. Symbols, visions, and apparitions will arise for your acceptance and understanding. They will dissolve and their energies will merge into your centre.

Remain calm and attentive.

What happens now is a succession of lights and sounds: the energetic forms of the different components of the Mind.

Accept the inner energies and resist all impulses to flee.

Recognise the visions as your own creation and know that they come from life experiences.

Think thus:

I AM the one who observes and accepts all that I perceive as a natural result
of the way I lived. A part of me is creating all this so that I may remember and
accept that I AM the totality of existence.

Light and Sound are two aspects of the same phenomenon. As such, strong, intensely resonating sounds will arise.

Remain in a state of neutrality. Emotions and sensations cannot harm you. Expand and assimilate the energies contained by the lights and sounds.

They are your own creation. You have the power to change your perception.

First Lapse

Different worlds or realities intertwine in a tumultuous whirl.

The space you find yourself in is a deep blue; the vibration of space you now feel is vast. It is the element ether, and within it, all substance, all matter arises.

Within this immense field of deepest blue, an enormous and radiant electric blue light approaches you with brilliant irradiation.

This blue represents your wise actions and dissolves all sense of a personal separate ego. It dissolves your limits.

It represents your Wisdom. Do not be afraid of it! Resist all desire to run away from yourself and from the fullness of the knowledge of your Being.

Remain serene. Accept and embrace what you are. Affirm the impulse that transcends the instincts you are now able to master.

Keep firm. Bathe yourself in the blue light. Delight in it. Be glad that you are being purified.

Resist any urge to flee.

Second Lapse

All kinds of images and sounds may arise. Observe everything impartially.

A white light now appears that represents fluidity and water. It corresponds to joy and the ability to create life forms.

This crystalline white light irradiates with an intense shine and transparency and seems to strike your heart.

Confront that white light and resist all rebelliousness — all pride or anger.

Have faith in that light; it is the light of Grace. Go within that light. It has the power to raise you to happiness.

Resist any desire to run away.

Third Lapse

The primitive form of the element earth now shines like a yellow irradiation. It represents feelings and sensations.

It is a period of intense flow of internal energy. Pulsate with it. It is what you experienced in freedom and equality with others.

Resist the temptation to run away or separate yourself through arrogance or disbelief.

Confront the magnificent transparent yellow light and blend with it as if with the Central Sun.

Do not surrender to sleep or drowsiness.

Fourth Lapse

Stay alert, stay centred. Focus. Nothing can distract you.

The form for the element fire now arises — pure and phosphorescent ruby light. It is discernment and intuition: passion for Truth.

Its colour reminds you of your own blood, the nourishment for your body. Blend with the fire flow of electrical intensity.

Firmly maintain yourself. Obey your Consciousness and resist any instinct that takes you away from it. You are noble. Affirm this nobility.

Confront the ruby light and recognise it as being an inner faculty of your own.

It represents Justice and discernment.

Dive into it as if you were diving into the true heart of the universe. Make an effort to stay aware.

Fifth Lapse

Now the element air appears. Nothing is solid. Waves of light and sound dance in confusion.

Remain alert, without distraction.

A green light appears, which represents the ability to think and act in harmony and with abnegation. It is the will to service and irradiates a brilliant, marvellous emerald green that flows like rings, which strike at your heart.

The radiant power of the green light is your ability to act harmoniously with the laws of the universe.

Resist envy and any feeling that is not in tune with this brilliant green light.

Delight and believe in this light. You will immerse yourself in the true Garden of Existence.

Resist any impulse to flee into comfortable inertia.

Sixth Lapse

You have gathered your energies, now purified by the different lights you have confronted. You have detached yourself from the reality you once knew…

Now all the lights appear simultaneously.

An explosion of lights, representing the five components of the conscious mind, shine intensely, striking out for you.

The irradiation from these lights is your own accumulation of good and purity: your ability to control and administer the different powers of your divine Self.

When you rejected those powers and the responsibilities related to them, you placed power outside, which now seeks to return to you.

Allow these energies and sensations to fuse into your heart.

Repeat internally:

I withdraw all power I gave to external things.
Confronting my fears and projections, I affirm:
I AM the activity of Cosmic Light and the
Purity of the powerful Sacred Fire within me.
I AM the Only Power acting!

Recognise your ability to project images. There is no need to run towards the lights or away from them. Don't allow for any feelings of self-pity or fear. Don't try to reach, hold onto, or attach yourself to anything. Allow yourself to know now what You Are and can be, as leader and mediator of men and women and as guardian of plants, animals, and life forces.

Seventh Lapse

As the energy accelerates and the primacy of memory imprints vie with cosmic forces of dissolution and regeneration, confusion intensifies.

Stay alert and centred, listening carefully.

It asks nothing of you and has nothing to do with you. Affirm Consciousness and control the automatic primitive instincts. Confront your responsibilities with enthusiasm, assume your powers, and exert the self-discipline that leads to true Freedom in the same proportion to the energy you now possess. You can do it.

Remember that you are capable of knowing and attracting in your direction the five radiant lights of wisdom and recognition.

Allow them to fuse into you. Fuse into them…

Eighth Lapse

A hurricane of activity now appears around you. The intensity of its voltage will be equal to how much of your once dispersed parts you were willing to accept, and it is here to distract and test you.

The mind will, at this point, continue to resist all the good it has accumulated with greater intensity.

The images you are confronted with are your own tendencies towards suppressed or expressed anger. Recognise and accept them without caring about the meaning implied. Integrate the opposites. Receive all Life: all you considered good together with all you considered bad.

Become aware of duality in action and remain apart from it. You are the Whole.

Acceptance is the power of life and its transmuting fire. This alchemy of transmutation is the key to eternal life.

Turning the Tide

This next stage marks a radical change in the way your Spirit asks you to respond.

You now find yourself in a transitional state between the formless state and the world of forms to which you currently belong and to which you are returning…

Your old ways, the egoism of the personality, may struggle to try to return. Be Still.

Resist any temptation — any feeling of attraction, repulsion, or curiosity — for now…

You are in a body because you want to be in a body. This body is your own creation and expresses your beliefs. It is extremely sensitive to vibrations, especially to your emotions.

Understand that your thought has phenomenal power in this moment and that it is capable of impressing your body and determining it.

You instantly create and attract that which you desire.

Use this faculty wisely.

Keep focused upon an image of Beauty and Perfection.

Choose the highest possible state of Consciousness.

Pray thus:

Divine Archangels, help me awaken
The unconscious parts of myself!
I, who am in reality Voidness,
The Source whence all things
are created.

Affirm:

I am a child of the Light
I love, live, and serve the Light
I am protected by the Light
I will live in a happy world
I abandon all ties and fear
I abandon desires and jealousy
I am reborn into the Light, into Love,
into Purity
I AM Light
I AM Love
I AM Purity

PART III: TRANSFORMATION OF CONSCIOUSNESS

Everywhere there is twilight — dim and diffuse. All things are familiar and yet… strange. Time extends into empty, grey spaces… All there is Time… endless time.

This is the moment to meditate on the quality of the Present. Feel its texture. Over this backdrop, physical realities are constructed. It feels like an extension of your own form that is thought-like, flowing…

Now deliberately evoke a Presence, a figure, a symbol, or a spiritual Path — something that inspires you, that offers you solace and hope…

Feel the Presence of your guides — beings who have accompanied you always and who love you. Maybe you never dared to feel them so clearly. Recognise your *Self*.

Sense them like the Presence of much-loved beings…

Now ask for the clarity you need to be guided on the right path.

And wait…

You find yourself in a transition between the formless state and the world of forms to which you belong and to which you are returning.

You are in a body of Light that resembles the one resting in the third dimension. It is extremely sensitive and impressionable to thoughts and emotions.

What you think becomes reality. Use this faculty wisely.

Hold your mind in a neutral state and without movement.

Resist the habits and impulses, the 'winds of karma', which are karmic patterns of attraction and repulsion, desire, and inclinations…

Concentrate exclusively on an image of beauty and perfection and on the sensation of being guided, loved, and supported.

Determine that you will be born into a healthy, prosperous, and productive world and reality. Choose the highest possible state of Consciousness for yourself.

Time seems eternal…

Everything is slow. Endless. Be still and wait.

To keep yourself focused, apply any formula or technique that has served you and inspires you: mantras, affirmations, prayer.

And wait for guidance. It always comes.

Feel the Presence of the Divine. The texture of intense quiet that emerges from your depths and which also surrounds you…

Honour God within and in all beings. Maintain this state and wait.

Pray thus:

Guides, Masters, Brotherhood of Light!
Help me remember my Self!
Help me find the appropriate rebirth, where
I may awaken the unconscious parts of myself!
I, who Am in reality the Void, the Source from
where all things are created.
The Void Clear Light!

Slowly and gradually, you are now, ever so carefully, journeying back into the initial frequency of the world you know.

Feel the pressure of the collective unconscious as you approach the denser astral climate of humanity as a whole…

Three powerful forces exert a tremendous attraction: anger, passion, and ignorance. Ignore them.

Become aware and keep your purpose in mind.

Resist the temptation to move or to agitate yourself. Instead, sustain a state of balance and neutrality. Remain in a state of serenity.

Affirm again and again:

I AM a Child of the Light.
I love, live, and serve the Light.
I am protected by the Light.
 will live in a happy world.

Meanwhile, you are more closely approaching the aura of collective humanity.

All past actions come up for review, the good with the bad. Lying is impossible.

You understand, forgive, and accept yourself, loving yourself in the way that you now feel you are truly loved.

Centre yourself exclusively on your Purpose.

This is a moment for containment of your activity and energy, a time for regeneration and accumulation of momentum. It is time for conscious choice.

Wait. Look. Feel. Accept.

Repeat to yourself:

I let go of all ties and fears.
I reiease all desire and jealousy.
I will live in Light, Love, and Righteousness.

PART IV: RESPONSIBILITY AND CHOICE

Stop working so hard in efforts that only perpetuate the illusions that keep you asleep.

Stop acting and reacting.

When there is no longer a struggle to be this or that, you will find yourself awake. You do not need to make an effort to awaken. (*May be repeated several times.*)

Affirm:

I AM the only Presence, the only power,
the only substance acting in my world!

The time for rebirth is arriving. You have the right to choose your life. Hold to the certainty that you will be surrounded by spiritually prepared beings.

Now, from the highest perspective of Love, Beauty, and Joy, enter into the light of the third dimension within the present Consciousness gradually.

Affirming:

I AM... I AM... I AM...
For always and forever I AM...
the only Presence, the only power,
the only Intelligence and substance
in action.

PART V: REBIRTH

As you are now at the height of clear intelligence, focused consciousness, and clear purpose, all you think will manifest.

Affirm:

I will live in a happy world: in harmony.
In a spiritual atmosphere of Light.
I Am a child of the Light.
I Am guided and protected by the Light.
I forever leave my past behind me.
I re-create myself in Light, in love, in purity.

Now act.

Visualise the subtle atoms of your body of Light re-creating an atmosphere of perfection.

Visualise and feel your emotional body re-creating itself in harmony — in peace, like a clear, tranquil lake.

Visualise and know that your mind re-creates itself with prime substance of golden light: a clean, clear mind that manifests the thought-forms of your Being.

Feel Earth's forces attracting and manifesting this perfection that you are now commanding.

Contemplate a healthy body… pure, fertile, tranquil emotions… a clear, clean mind…

Impress these forms — this healthy body of physical perfection, this peaceful, centred emotional body and this clarified mind — over your earthly form.

Now, approach your body softly… with respect and gratitude.

In your body of Light, enter into your physical body and fill it with this new frequency, with this new energy re-created in Consciousness. Your actual physical body remains serene and poised, perfectly still, as yet uninhabited by the fullness of your Consciousness.

Now!

Feel the energy of life, of rebirth, entering into the atoms of the physical body, re-creating itself in Light. Feel the glory of rebirth as a man-god: the seedling of God awakened in you.

Affirm:

I AM. I AM Light.
I Am Light in matter and,
As of this moment, I honour this Light!

Sense Consciousness awakening sweetly within the cells, the bones, the muscles… Lovingly occupy the space of this physical form, feeling it breathe and vibrate with the frequencies of a new life.

What you are feeling in your psycho-physical mechanism is energy.

Use your intelligence and remember:

Each thought qualifies this energy and gives it form.

Take yourself by the hand, and, as if you were a child, tell your body it is loved and protected. Repeat it until all of you fully believe it.

This is the precise moment of re-creation.

I AM loved and protected.

Keep your consciousness as a Being in the most sublime state of purity and joy possible.

You are Light, you are Love, you are Pure Consciousness and Intelligence!

You are Unique in the Universe of Sentient Beings.

Enjoy it! Expand your Light. Expand your Being.

You... you who are an expression of the Infinite! Unrepeatable.

Unique. Perfect.

PART VI: POST RE-CREATION

Renouncing the attachments to your former identity, affirm:

I AM Light.
Forever and for all time, I AM...
The only Presence, the only power,
The only Intelligence and substance
Acting in my world.

Do not allow doubt or fear to enter.
Affirm:

I will live in a happy world.
I seek harmony.
I seek a spiritual atmosphere of Light.
I Am a child of the Light.
I Am guided and protected by the Light.
I forever abandon my past, my fears, my doubts, my jealousies, and my desires.
I re-create myself in Light, in Love, in Purity.
I AM Light.
I AM Love.
I AM Purity.

Feel the Earth's forces attracting this perfection into your body.

Recognise the Threefold Unfed Flame around your physical body and surrounding it like a protective mantle.

Your entire right side is covered by an intense blue irradiation with crystalline specks.

The Threefold Flame © Stéphane Dubois 2023

Your entire left side is covered by an intense pink irradiation speckled with gold.

Your entire front, from head to toe, is covered by a fine golden irradiation…

Feel the energy of life, of rebirth, entering into the atoms of the physical body and re-creating itself in Light.

Feel the peace, the new life, the harmony, the beauty of the substance of your body, of your mind, and of your emotions.

Breathe this new life into your body.

Feel the glory of rebirth, like the seedling of God awakening in you.

Sense your newborn body completely enfolded by the Threefold Flame which, like tender flower petals, protects the sweet seed of life engendered in Light.

Be whole. Be free.

Use your divine gifts of manifestation to inspire and construct a better world for everyone.

RENOVATION

Once you have completed the ego-death process, you have crossed the threshold that separated you from the Real, but you still need to integrate that new perspective and apply it in your life. Pay close attention to your honed faculties and powers, or you may re-create or fall into the clutches of old habits and tendencies of the past.

After experiencing the *Bardo*, your first impression upon waking and returning to third-dimensional reality is usually one of serene amazement; you know you have gone through something so profound that it transcends the intellect and all sensations. There is now also something implanted in your heart that is familiar and very pleasant to you — like a great secret that gives you tremendous pleasure. It's a magic key, although you still don't know how it works.

Above and beyond any doubt or fear, you now feel that you carry great love and deep security within you; whatever happens, you know yourself as strong and confident. You can now favourably transform any situation so that defeat or negativity are things you can no longer conceive. Since you have been through death and know it does not exist, your heart is charged with power and hope.

When you've already been to the top of the mountain, you don't settle for a partial view of the valley. You know yourself and, with practice, can re-create that state of union needed to access whatever knowledge you're seeking and to acquire the necessary strength for your life projects. When you approach a goal in this state, success is inevitable.

It is a new beginning. You are now fully aware that personally focused 'normal' life, as you knew it, is in conflict with spiritual life, and that embracing the latter appeals to you more. You can see that each person is unique and has come equipped with particular gifts and desires that will develop in a certain way. This difference stimulates the effort that will generate joy and transcendence. Spirituality is not *what* you do but *how* you do what you do: in other words, the level of Consciousness with which you act in your day-to-day life.

So, the task now is to update the structure of your personality. Imagine that you are a house, and, over the years, you must review and modernise your surroundings, renovating floors, walls, and electrical systems. You will make sure everything is in the best condition, fixing what is stuck, using new materials to replace what doesn't work, eliminating what is no longer important, and upgrading what remains through new purchases or redecoration. In other words, you'll do everything necessary to maintain the new environment dictated by the Spirit that now fills you.

Meanwhile, the energy that moves you is phenomenal. What will you do with that energy? How will you manage it? Your perception, intelligence, and faculties are at their best, but the body — and quite possibly the personality — still won't know how to handle the changes.

Following such a dramatic change, until balance is naturally established, there is a human tendency to get rid of things: leave work, throw old clothes in the trash, change or move furniture, or even leave your partner. But beware: that's not change! It's a reaction. In other words, it just means more of the same.

Real change involves maturity, discernment, and sustainment, not impulsivity or escapism.

What the cycle of humanity demands today in all areas — from politics and economics to relationships and sexuality — is the creation of new forms, because the world demands novelty. Whether you are content with a superficial change or wish to provoke a radical one, you will soon discover that you are drowning — an experience further intensified by your newly heightened awareness.

After ego-death, just as in a new life, there is learning, exploration, and adaptation.

For at least three months, you may go through a phase of trial and error: making mistakes, feeling anaesthetised, resisting, getting angry, or even depressed, and you may forget about yourself in multiple ways — constantly correcting things and falling repeatedly into self-indulgence. But every time, you will get back up. Such is the choreography of this world!

——
Spirituality is not what you do but how you do what you do: in other words, the level of Consciousness with which you act in your day-to-day life.
——

Learn what a mistake is, what humility is (which leads you to recognise it), and what it means to exercise the muscle of self-discipline.

Without shame, deception, or euphemisms, affirm what is in you. Remember that you have phenomenal faculties; some of them are offered to you more readily than to others. The important thing is that you know this and start seeing the self-sabotage that remains. Deception is not possible because now everything bounces off you.

Simplify. You already know that for you there are limitations. Recognise what your style is, what you do well, and how you do it. You must restructure your personality, forging the character of a disciple. This involves relying on the faculties and powers you know you have, identifying your limitations, and being flexible — ultimately relying on your strengths to balance your weaknesses.

Keep examining those ideas within society that you still support without thinking. Don't try the impossible. Wanting to be what you are not creates a tension that will block you and take you away from what is rightfully yours: happiness. Work with what you have and be happy. If others don't see you or don't want to grow with you, you shouldn't care. You can only do your part.

NEW LIFE CONTRACTS

What do you want out of life?
What kind of life do you want to live from now on?
How do you want to live it?

Make a list of all your essential and non-essential aspirations, which are equally important, and start manifesting them. Think of these as New Life Contracts that will replace the old contracts that determined your previous life. Remember that a life without challenges or pleasures is boring. You need something to keep you alert and awake. You could like comfort, but you don't want a cushy life. When you desire a relationship, it is to grow. The primary relationship you know now is with yourself. Describe in your mind exactly how you will need your spirit to express itself fully, prepare for it, and attract it. Your desire and joyful Presence releases the energy of Source for you. Manifest what you have inside as only you can.

Your longing reveals and determines what you were born for, where and how you were born: whether an artist, scientist, businessman/woman, dedicated mother, social worker, doctor, lawyer, shoe shiner, coal miner, or computer technician. You must live the relationship, fulfil the desires you hold, have the child you want, be successful, and schedule the ideal retirement — unless, perhaps, you do not seek any of that. Nothing you do or fail to do will tarnish the quality of your Being as you live the life you have chosen. It will be the reflection of *who* you are and *what* you always have been. For you are a spiritual being in a body of matter, and everything is spiritual.

You will continue to elaborate on your personality. It is your Great Work, and you now have your whole life to dedicate to it. Your tools are your intellectual and emotional skills (which are different for everyone). So begin to notice how your intellect works, how your emotional body works, and discover your physical vitality. Do not attempt gymnastics if your basic rhythm is gentle and delicate. Nor should you do yoga if you're a gymnast; it won't match your temperament. By the same token, develop flexibility and don't limit yourself to only *one* type of activity.

Stop energising fear; it no longer serves as an excuse. Fear is a ghost — it's not real! Your mind creates it and looks for ways to justify it. Your highest priorities should be the mastery of your emotions, your impulses, and your body. The ideal is a fair and neutral perception that rests in a healthy physical body. Your body generates vitality, emotions qualify your energies, and the mind motivates and drives you.

The correction you must make requires careful, objective, intelligent analysis and sensitivity. Remember that real Intelligence is not automatic or intellectual; instead, feel the quality of your Intelligence. During moments of confusion, sit and breathe, find out what is behind that which disturbs you, eliminate external influences, and allow yourself to *know*. Permit yourself to *know* and remember to take the necessary time. The most natural thing is for you to sit with your Presence, with your guides, with your Intelligence, and let them reveal to you what you need. The least natural is what you did before: permitting your mind to turn around and around while telling yourself you are stupid and asking others to think or do things for you.

Stop energising fear; it no longer serves as an excuse. Fear is a ghost — it's not real!

To *do* is not to *be*. Your doing should be based on what you are being: on what you affirm that you are, on the prime use of your faculties and your powers, on the focus of your Intelligence, and the management of your energies. When you want to change your world, first look at yourself and your level of Consciousness, because the result will depend on that.

You are perfect. When you thought you were imperfect, you created flawed patterns of expression that validated this initial belief. If you expect adversity, you will get it, but if you recognise yourself fully, the world will reflect abundance back to you.

Your world always mirrors you. Remember this. If you lose the face of your beauty, FIND IT again. Look into the mirror, past all those haunting ghosts of thought-forms that have no more place in your life… and find the ANGEL. Find YOURSELF.

PART FIVE

KARMA AND THE DEATH PROCESS

There are people who think that in some space of infinity, up or out there, there are lords who will judge us in death, making us pay for all the evils and omissions we have committed, or reward us for how good we have been. We project a whole hierarchy of masters who decide for us.

ZULMA REYO, *Inner Alchemy*

The Experience During Karma

The remainder of this book addresses wisdom that can assist in a deeper inner understanding of both the ego-death and physical death process. I focus first on the karmic process as described by the Tibetan school.

THE KARMIC WHEEL

As mentioned previously, there is nothing outside that is not inside. In truth, there is nobody 'out there'. It is possible to assume that these apparently external judges exist through a partial understanding of the Karmic Board, in which there are teachers, guides, and masters representing each one of the rays of life energy used or misused by us in our lifetime.[10] Here, it is very important not to forget that you are ONE with THE ALL. In that sense, it is you — you are one with the teachers, guides, and masters. For this reason, you cannot argue or lie to yourself.

One of the more subtle and commonplace roles we revert to in life is that of the victim. In other words, we adopt the toxic stance of the 'wounded one' in the face of pain and abuse. At one level, we know perfectly well what we are doing when we choose this role. It is easier to blame others for our terrible situation than to assume the tremendous responsibility of having attracted this circumstance for ourselves. We all suffer pain and abuse in this lifetime; however, it remains our choice to be a powerless victim or to rise above.

Sadly, life is not all fun and games. You didn't come here to have a good time or simply to be happy: this is an illusion fostered repeatedly throughout all cultures, past and present. Real happiness is of another sort.

In truth, you are a master, whose task is to learn further mastery over matter by providing an example and being in service to life, that life becomes a unity, a One-ness, in harmony with greater Life. Life owes you nothing; it is you who owes life.

Unless this is realised and understood, humanity will continue to promulgate today's broken world.

You can choose to be part of the ongoing spiritual evolution of humankind. You already see the beginning of a better world; with effort, dedication, and focus in whatever way you can best serve, you could be the one to plant the seeds and build it as a physical reality

> Life owes you nothing; it is you who owes life. Unless this is realised and understood, humanity will continue to promulgate today's broken world.

10 See *Inner Alchemy* for more information on the rays of life energy.

The Karmic Wheel

— elevating every field of human endeavour. This is the opposite of victimisation: the sooner you can understand the nature of the wounds within and transmute them, the sooner you will find your true power and purpose. Dimensional awareness will light your way. By continuing to use the perspectives attained through the *Alchemical Alignment*, you can go to those levels, ask for what you need, and receive the necessary information. You, in your wholeness, have that power.

In the physical dying process, you are confronted with a series of symbols that will test you in an energetic sense. Light and sound, the most universal languages, will appear before you and within you. The cloak of density that covers you here on Earth prevents you from experiencing the new forces of life right now, but in death, you will sense them and experience them clearly.

The purpose of this testing is to learn to administrate life's energies, forces, and faculties ethically, in tune with the One.

It is not so much what you see but what you discover emotionally that could cause you regrets. If you have not developed your faculties of sensitivity, or if you have abused your gifts, you will feel guilty.

In death you are helpless; there is no insulation and nothing external to protect you. You come into direct contact with the dynamics of Creation itself. You are used to pulling on the protective covers of isolation and remaining in your safe place. However, the knowledge of the process outlined here grants power to those who understand the mechanics of thought management and creation. It is your responsibility to learn and discover this knowledge in your depths and become exemplars of this teaching, inspiring and encouraging others to rise into the glory and profundity of life. In mastery, this teaching empowers us to rise to our full height.

May you recognise the tremendous Light within and affirm:

'I Am the Power of the Light!'

When you love the whole of who you are, you are full and without dependency. You are in yourself, and this is the place where people can come together in genuine relationships to serve in a way that makes a difference in the world.

If you are in that place of strength and power, you will inspire others. You attract what you are.

THE BARDO

As we look back at the full text of the *Bardo*, we understand its parts.

Having cleared the way to *becoming* through the ego-death, you were ready to look at the *Bardo*, which is the second experience in the Trajectory of Consciousness. In the Tibetan version of the *Bardo*, the way beyond appears as temptations, precipices, and places where you may hide from yourself. This is the stage where many people fall, especially those

The Reality of the Mind

who have not learned the truth surrounding the death process and the responsibility of the Self.

In your everyday life, you face similar temptations to avoid facing the painful consequences of your actions and, instead, seek comfort and oblivion. Likewise, in the *Bardo,* at this point, you descend into an automatic incarnation or situation that mirrors exactly what you are running away from. If you do not face your responsibility in this world, on Earth, you will attract similar or worse conditions again and again. There is no escape possible from your Spirit-self.

This is the experience where you will face the Reality of the Mind.

> If you do not face your responsibility in this world, on Earth, you will attract similar or worse conditions again and again. There is no escape possible from your Spirit-self.

THE REALITY OF THE MIND

The Reality of the Mind is revealed symbolically throughout most of your journey Home as an internal review of your mental pursuits. The memory of all life is played back in images and sensations as a summary of everything that has happened to you.

The experience is like the play-back of a film, as light unwinds all the imprints to recapitulate your existence. Sounds will accompany the actions, powers, and tendencies of your life — in particular, the projections of desires and aversions.

To the one who has already prepared, it will not be difficult to confront them and rescue the power and purity within each life force.

THE FORCES OF LIGHT

The Forces of Light in the *Bardo* represent not only the positive aspects of the indwelling essence of life qualities and faculties but also the reactionary aspects. Bright colours appear in all their shining glory and are extremely intense. However, if you have not mastered the life lessons that each of them has to offer, their purity will deflect you towards the lesser light that defines an inferior world.

The following illustration summarises the positive and reactionary aspects of the Five Pure Lights and their combination in the Rainbow that you experience in the *Bardo.* Each Pure Light is represented by the material world elements of air, water, fire, and earth along with ether (or aether), the fifth element (or quintessence), and the material that fills the region beyond Earth. Then there is the Rainbow: a combination of all the lights.

Indigo Blue is Ether

Its positive aspect represents Wisdom, Equanimity, Benevolence, and the Integration of the Self. Its reactionary expression appears as matte white light emanating from the egoic centre and manifesting the feeling of separation from everything and everyone.

Crystal White is Water

Its positive aspect is the Creator of order and forms of life, happiness, and fulfilment. It is personified as a Leader, a Mediator or a wise Warrior. In its reactionary expression, it appears as leaden grey light — the centre of violence and hatred. It depicts the murderer or victim: the inhabitants of infernal worlds.

Shiny Yellow is the Earth

With tolerance for all human beings as its positive aspect, it is loving, understanding, and fair. Arrogance, pride, and aloofness are its reactionary aspects, as revealed in a smoky blue-green light.

Ruby Red is Fire

It represents pure discernment in its positive aspect, as shown through the highest levels of perception. Conversely, all fears and regrets, unquenchable desires and passions, unbearable longings and attachments are represented in its reactionary aspects. This is the world of the starving gods and manifests in an opaque brick-red light.

Emerald Green is Air

It represents perfected reason and the ability to act and work generously for the good of all. Its reactionary expression is consumed with greed, possessiveness, and is the world of the jealous gods, the 'asuras', perceived as opaque matte-green light.

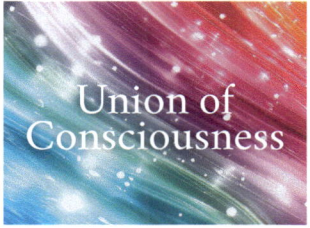

The Rainbow represents the union of Consciousness

All positive aspects of Light fully integrated in perfect wisdom. In contrast, the absence of the rainbow is darkness — full of ignorance and unconsciousness, where the base instincts dominate in the world of brute forces.

For the one who has not prepared beforehand, this experience of the *Pure Lights* will be revelatory. The shell of your material incarnation can no longer protect you from the reality of who you really are, as you are stripped of all the illusions and artificial edifices of the personality you have created. These traits will be self-reviewed and either found to be wanting or resolved. The aspects of your Self revealed in *The Reality of the Mind* will be taken with you into your next incarnation.

ONE WITH GOD

On the other hand, if you have done the hard work of the ego-death in this incarnation and know that God is One with you, and you are One with God, (or The Divine, Divinity, or Godliness), you are aware of the reality of your Spirit-Self. At this point, as a matter of self-preservation and accumulation of force, it is vital to resist the longing to move towards or away from anything. You simply stay put until the work here in the *Bardo* is done. This means holding a state of Presence.

Many ancient traditions such as mystic Christianity, ancient Egyptian, esoteric Judaism, Hinduism, and Tibetan Buddhism teach the habit of meditating and evoking formulae that sustain a state of Presence. If you come from such a tradition, these prayers or meditations are ingrained in you. If not, then I recommend the following affirmation that I included in *Inner Alchemy*:

I am a child of the Light. I live in the Light. I love the Light. I serve the Light. I am guided and protected by the Light. I bless the Light.

This is an example of a decree or affirmation that will hold you fast. It goes deeply into the soul. This is the time to hold on to your truth, which will assist in leading you to your Renaissance or Rebirth in Light.

> Many ancient traditions such as mystic Christianity, ancient Egyptian, esoteric Judaism, Hinduism, and Tibetan Buddhism teach the habit of meditating and evoking formulae that sustain a state of Presence.

RENAISSANCE AND REBIRTH

Renaissance is the third experience in the Trajectory of Consciousness. Here, you learn the use of effort and the process of discernment in the reformation of Consciousness. In this experience, the old ego tries to return, and you go through the test of resisting old karmic impulses, much of which relate to an understanding of the power of desire.

DESIRE

Your Renaissance, or Rebirth, is determined by the vibratory frequency of your desire. This is an extremely important yet difficult concept for most people to grasp. As previously mentioned, during the potentially long period in the *Bardo*, where you face the Light of Truth and Love in the ego-death, you will attract what you are afraid of or desire.

Whatever you are thinking of or aspiring towards serves as a focus for your nature in your re-embodiment, whether driven by your greatest fears or simplest desires. So it is important to remember that:

You create your own reality.

If you have the appropriate spiritual discipline and stamina, this can be determined consciously or in your rebirth. You will be led unconsciously by whatever you have failed to deal with in the ego-death stage of the *Bardo*.

You attract exactly what you are afraid of or desire.

Desire will lead you in one way or another, and here is its artful use. Consciously, you can hold in mind the type of life and the kind of world you want. It becomes imprinted upon the life-stirring ethers of *becoming* in that fertile moment.

This can be supported by a prayer or mantra or whatever comes naturally: the evoked embrace of your Guardian Angel behind you, the acknowledgement of your Angel-Self, or an image of a sun or flower in the heart for inspiration.

This is a conscious process of selection and discernment, where you determine what matters most to you. The old ego will try until the very end to test the residue karmic impulses, so you must remain firm throughout.

KARMIC IMPULSES

This is a topic we should now explore in more detail. Like each of us, you have your own particular karmic impulses, which have arisen throughout your present incarnation as an inclination towards one thing or against another. For instance, if you tend to be lazy, then laziness will show up and drive you during your renaissance or rebirth. This could even manifest as the desire for death to be eternal sleep.

The karmic impulse — that habit you created in your separation state — will constantly come back and test you. Even resentment can return, which is why so many ancient religious traditions emphasise forgiveness — even of our worst enemies. And all the pain that occurred in this and previous lives must be released.

You may ask, how can I forgive a mass murderer? Providing that you are not blinded by pain and rage, you may begin to understand where the forces that drive such a person to commit dreadful deeds came from; perhaps, then, you'll be able to generate love, compassion, and forgiveness. The energy generated by forgiveness forms a field of compassion that will surround that person until, at some future time, they allow it in and achieve redemption.

Anger creates a shell, as does fear. You must identify yours.

Each one of your karmic tendencies creates a shell around you; altogether, they can create a blockage that nothing can pierce and which even the grace that constantly flows from Source cannot easily penetrate. This explains why people ask, 'Where is God? I call for God but there is no help'. The answer is that nobody can help you if you are not open to that help or are holding a grudge around you. You may be so fixed in your own defence that you cannot accept the grace that is always available.

LETTING GO AND ATTRACTING POSITIVE ENERGY

The Renaissance, or Rebirth in the afterlife, is an opportunity to let go of fears and desires and is also a means of attracting and anchoring the energies you want to cultivate in your future life. This is the time to regenerate, to withdraw, and to choose intelligently. It's also an opportunity to re-examine the contract between your physical body and the Earth, which lends you its textures to build and sustain your physical body.

The energy generated by forgiveness forms a field of compassion that will surround that person until, at some future time, they allow it in and achieve redemption.

When the physical body has been cleansed because you are spiritually awake, in the process of ego-death you behold your body with compassion. This is the time for appreciation of all the beauty and perfection it offers. This is the moment to bless it and heal it, a moment of gratitude for the opportunity of embodiment. You may affirm:

I will come back into a healthy and flexible emotional, mental, and physical body.

You can choose to re-enter in a clear and lucid mental framework, joining with the perfection inside the body — your Spirit-Self — to imprint the physical self with a new pattern.

It is up to you to use what you have learned and to remember and hold the purest and most perfect image that is true to your Spirit-Self.

Your Spirit-Self only wants beauty and perfection for you. It will give you all the tools you need to manifest these qualities if you only pause in stillness and silence long enough. There is a whole hierarchy of souls to help you, such as your immediate Teacher or Guide, along with instructors and friends acting under this Guide. Then there are the people like yourself, who come close to you, but are not in a physical body — all feeling and hoping for your success. And there are also those who are learning to teach, just like you. All these souls will strive to help and guide you.

—

Your Spirit-Self only wants beauty and perfection for you. It will give you all the tools you need to manifest these qualities if you only pause in stillness and silence long enough.

—

DISCERNMENT AND DEVELOPMENT

During the *Bardo* experience, you understood, albeit subliminally, what the forces are that lie within you and that you can access through Intelligence-Presence. Now it is a question of reinforcing the inner vision that is directed more towards globality than to the details or fragments of reality, more towards potentiality and origin than to the aspects of manifested plurality.

Now that you intuit how these elements determine your tangible physical world, you have grasped the essence of the great law of manifestation:

You create what you conceive in the proportion,
and at the level, that you believe and affirm it.

Every manifestation starts from the administration and modulation of your energies or powers. Ideal conditions arise from emotional stability and the power of conviction.

From now on, your life can become a conscious and deliberate act. You have the ability to perceive and construct realities. The best tool you have is the *Alchemical Alignment*, rising to the experience of the Solar Electronic Presence and accessing the highest possible energy frequency for your own being and world. From that perspective, while maintaining balance on a physical and psychological level, you can visualise and affirm what you wish to manifest without giving space to fear or doubt.

In relationships, the *Alchemical Alignment* will allow you to see others neutrally. This helps you to prevail in your Consciousness and to inhabit your real identity beyond the personality and its effects. You cannot change anyone or anything other than yourself, but you can attract the good and the productive, avoid confusion, and discern what works and what does not. This requires perseverance, diligence, practice, and, above all, patience.

Apply this alignment first to yourself and then to your relationships; others will respond to how you see them. Recognise both the personality and the essence of the other, being cautious with the first and trusting in the second.

Releasing the past is meaningless if you do not discover what it is to live in the present. Mere dominion of the mind is not sufficient to bring about change — thought must connect with bodily vitality and feelings if you are to manifest the frequency you are seeking.

The basic dynamic is one of affirmation, along with the deliberate and conscious modulation of emotional and mental energies in harmony.

If you are to avoid falling back into the patterns of the Wheel of Karma, you must follow a Purpose. It is naïve and arrogant to believe that you are capable of doing anything you want simply because your heart is pure. The mind must be trained to obey the impulse of Higher Intelligence rather than the senses. Your goal is to sustain perception on a higher neutral plane so that you can access and use your real Intelligence as Consciousness.

> Recognise both the personality and the essence of the other, being cautious with the first and trusting in the second.

REINCARNATION

Reincarnation defines the entry point when you come back into your body and fill it with the grace of life from Source. This is when you breathe and implant the thoughts you have set in the Renaissance stage of the *Bardo*. It requires energy mastery. Your task is to maintain continuous positive stability, without attraction or repulsion, while keeping the mind and emotions fixed in the final act of self re-creation, as described above.

 ### FLIGHT OF LOVE: A MEDITATION ON DESIRE
The following meditation can be used as an aid to working with and redirecting positive desires after the ego-death process.

It all begins in the Mother of all things as Feeling
Vision without centre
fathomless possibility

streaming into
a journey of Love-Desire
shaft of limitless diamond light
gauze-like shades of colour
breathing
falling in delightful rhythm
forms intensely
pulsing
nothingness and all
as yet unknowing

Maelstrom
eternal centre and periphery
expressing
Being
coordinating
diaphanous accords
amplitude, rhythmic cadences
perception of multiplicity
shades of light

resonance
perennial relationship
manifesting

Coalescence
reproducing and attuning
this and that
infinite options
Will to Be as longing
versions of Self as different tastes
extending and contracting
space created
by a sigh
transformation, satisfaction and pleasure
aspiration
a game sparkling in a pocket deep inside, concealed

INCARNATION

Diving into concave emptiness
landing
immersed in textures of Earth
a world designed
ecstasy of dance and newborn senses
transporting, manifesting
formulating
becoming thought
mind unfolds
in shapes of longing
feeling
weaving

Mother-Feeling spills into song
harmonious impressions
subliminal experience
sustained in apparent continuity
generating a wealth of possibility
abundance, strength

refining, preserving, elevating
dipping again
primal fluidity
matter-space, infinite resource
works of art
diversity, polarities reflect, giving birth to selves

The body
tangible product of inspiration
consumes
re-creates
liberates itself
only to create
more bonds
combining faculties
reproducing and evoking soul experience
each moment and every breath
reality
one power evokes a greater one

Miniscule artifices conjure
allied forces of earth, water
fire and air.
each
a universe
together
a galaxy
within-without
the initial journey echoing
in structures, rhythms
and unimaginable universes
discovering themselves within

Heart, centre of Creation
obedient
Solar Principle
fixing illusions

identities
adapting and applying
weaving Maya
shimmering fascinations
set to intimate patterns
humanity
acquiring one focus and another
the separate and the distinct

the Force drives
commanding, dominating
playing
at being commanded, dominated
bodies attract but do not fuse
resonances alter without living the symphony
until exhausted
appearance of concretion
slides into the waters of the Source
perennial home
eternal Consciousness
rebirth

FULLNESS, SOUL EXPRESSION

Original Sentient Intelligence
dressed in myriad transparencies
as many shapes, deep
ample, flexible
Mother-Feeling knits manifestation from Itself
sustaining soul
Being
architect of worlds
personal will, divine Will
tangible impulse of supreme Power
linearity marries concentricity
coordination reigns

I AM all. One. Unity.

In equilibrium, serenity
congruence
Life centre
expands
perfect affinity with lunar force
what is Above is that which is Below
primal matter without tension
flows in living currents
instinctive access to Source
endlessly reborn
the Plan is done

Coordination, unity of purpose
Creation
dissolving space and time
in particles
freedom, wholeness
Desire and Power
peak
by feeling
Feeling
Love by loving
rest in perfect Peace
as in the Beginning but different.

PART SIX

APPENDIX

Most traditions have taught that there is but one Truth and that it is both Intelligence and Love: the great cohesive forces of creation. Likewise, there is one Presence, one Higher Intelligence, one power: absolute infinite reality.

From a purely material perspective, this has been called 'no-thing-ness', yet from the perspective of Consciousness, this same reality is 'every-thing-ness' — *all that is*. In other words, this sublime reality is not just another thing among many others but also the very Being that gives Being to all creation.

Consciousness is the subtle crowning frequency of Intelligence. When embodied, it is encapsulated in slower, denser rhythms and gives life, Intelligence, and inspiration to the matter it creates and inhabits. Each lifetime is granted a different duration within a specific body for the purpose of learning, redemption, teaching, or simply for rest and play. During deep sleep, if unencumbered by personal preoccupations, souls venture upwards to whatever dimensional level they have earned through their evolution and then, upon awakening, they return to the third dimension. In other words, sleep is a small death. Similarly, every intense peak experience, such as joy, shock, pain, fright, or excitement reveals degrees of energetic intensity that spark an increase in the vibratory frequency beyond their usual rhythm in matter.

It is important to remember that the personality is distinct from the soul. The soul signifies the totality of integrated life lessons learned while embodied; it is suffused with Intelligence through its exposure to higher spheres. The personality, by contrast, is a temporary creation of the soul and is linked to only one particular lifetime, purpose, and mission. The experiences of physical death refer mainly to the personality. During the process, the soul simply waits for the personality to disentangle itself from its self-created identity and has little to do until the moment of re-embodiment. If and when the personality becomes infused with soul qualifications, it relinquishes its self-created identity from the burdensome bonds of matter to live and work from higher dimensional perspectives. This equates to the third phase of the dying process.

The ancients knew this. For instance, the Egyptians believed that, at death, the deceased's heart was weighed against a feather on the scale of Maat (Justice). If the heart weighed more than the feather, that person could not pass into the freedom of the spirit world but must remain wandering in the subworld until the extra weight and density dissolved.

—

Consciousness is the subtle crowning frequency of Intelligence. When embodied, it is encapsulated in slower, denser rhythms and gives life, Intelligence, and inspiration to the matter it creates and inhabits.

—

In the East, this weight is called karma. In Christianity, it is identified with the sins that create hell. The only way to ease this situation is by withdrawing the energies deposited in attachments to matter. That's because, when we die, the only things that truly 'die' are our creations — the accumulated personal desires and fears of a lifetime. In other words, earth must return to earth and Consciousness to the Absolute.

THE ANCIENT VIEW OF REALITY

Ancient texts on death relate creation to the dynamics of human life, helping us recognise the difference between Consciousness and the substance (matter) it wears in embodiment. The mechanical structure of the human being is understood to be composed of various forces and energies interacting at the multiple planes of the universe.

Because most of humanity lives without knowledge of essential Truth, especially the aspect of recognising their own Spirit as Source, they believe they need someone or something external to grant them the power and authority they think they lack. That's why, in order to reach people at different levels of understanding, much of the training for death originally alluded to an intermediary, such as a religious tradition, guru, shaman, or some other means to respond to the deceased's needs and provide guidance, hope and strength. For some, in life, as in death, this appears as an angel who keeps a record of every human thought, feeling, and action. However, for those who are prepared, it is the soul itself that appears — the innermost voice that perpetually reminds one 'I AM that I AM'.

The ancient world thought very differently from how we do today. For them, there existed no real concept of a subjective personal world or an intellectual bent of mind, nor was there the same overwhelming demand for privacy from the chaos that dominates our daily lives. They instead spent their time studying forces, energies, and correspondence between the stars, alongside the principles of sacred architecture and the science of manifestation and dematerialisation. To them, these were as important and real as anatomy and physiology are to us today. These cultures, which included the Egyptians, Vedic Indians, Mesoamericans, and those indigenous to the three Americas, understood the energy structure of the body and mind and its kinship to cosmology. Unlike modern society, their intelligence was holistic, analogical, and conceptual. By contrast, today we are more analytic, categorical, and personalistic.

As a consequence of the all-absorbing experience of matter, the ancients transmitted Truth sensorially through resonance and energetic impregnations of material objects. For instance, they built temples in synchronicity with geodesic lines that aligned with the stars. The various gods that populated these temples symbolised the elemental forces of the animal and mineral kingdoms as seen in their architecture. The elements and other natural forces became the 'Neters' or the various gods. The Kingdom of Egypt saw itself as a single body with one established purpose: to provide a prototype for universal teaching, similar to those provided in the East in previous Indian Vedic cycles. Although the surviving Egyptian texts, which became the basis of Western history, remain fragmentary, they are enough to excite our intuition. Similar teachings were planted in the Americas at the same time. The power garnered and emitted from those times is enormous and survives to the present day.

Today, when only one person is in alignment with their higher dimensional Self and connected with Truth, the effect is exponential. When a whole group focuses on an Ideal, they are capable of working at multiple levels, equal to what was attained by the Egyptians. In ancient times, such abilities included the supra-mental practice of the constructing and implanting of reality. Before crafting matter into its particular form, a subtle mould made of mental substance (rather than physical) was projected at very high frequencies — a practice supported by stellar and earthly forces. Even after thousands of years, these frequencies still exude from the stone structures they left behind. Physical matter may decay, but the etheric substance that underlies the material does not. The same thing happens when we die; just like the emissions from these temples, the frequencies of human life continue to resonate after the separation and decay of the physical form.

Along these lines, the ancients paved the way to identifying and administering life forces through their rigorous observations of the world. Impressions, memories, and even beliefs were, for them, a tangible reality that could be sensed, and their creations at the material third dimension became the place to study such phenomena. Their initiation centres, also known as Mystery Schools, were places where one learned to utilise the power of mind as Higher Intelligence. There, students

—

When a whole group focuses on an Ideal, they are capable of working at multiple levels, equal to what was attained by the Egyptians.

—

discovered their own capacity to evoke and imprint forms with life force and so carry on the secrets known to these civilisations. This is one of the purposes of our own Inner Alchemy School of Consciousness.

THE ANCIENT EGYPTIANS

The ancient Egyptian civilisation was constructed with an awareness of the dynamics of the higher dimensions. The living were given instructions on how to live in the greater universe, and the dead were offered rituals and warnings. Their book for the dead, *The Book of Life*, shows they understood the aspects of physical, astral, and spiritual life. The latter books of this compendium map out the unity of our lives with the solar and lunar universe. In other words, the individual (as well as the planet) reflected the whole cosmos, which was mirrored in man and woman. Personal

The Egyptians

consciousness was determined by cosmological, astronomical, and natural laws. This, in turn, minimised the impact of divergent personal wills.

Another seminal text, *The Egyptian Book of the Dead*, consists of eight volumes composed at different moments during its rich ancient history. Each one is filled with highly complex rituals that represent distinct phases through which human consciousness must pass. Its symbolism differs from its Tibetan equivalent, since its mission was to teach all humanity, not just an elite few.

The initial phase, described in the first volume, consists of invoking names of power for every aspect of natural and cosmic life (in *Inner Alchemy,* this stage is simplified by repeatedly evoking the *Alchemical Alignment*). This period covers the first four or five days of work.

The second phase, found in the *Book of Caverns*, speaks of the six processes or transformations in the history of Osiris, the divine-human model. This stage is the moment where the power of Light — which transforms and regenerates dense matter — is recovered. Together, these two phases represent the passage from the tomb to the sun or Source. They illustrate the journey of death and rebirth in its entirety — a journey from a normal life of relationships to one of future possibilities.

The next two volumes focus mainly on cosmology. With rare exceptions, there is no place for this sort of expertise in our society, conditioned as it is by a frantic sense of haste. In our own work, these phases are not covered except for some occasional allusions.

Volume three describes various doors and barriers Spirit must encounter on its journey. Coursing through a celestial river, Spirit passes through twelve doors guarded by snakes, which are symbols of wisdom, and their respective temptations. Beginning in the West, a region of death and darkness, it continues through experiences represented by four archetypes: Ra, Set, Horus, and Sekhmet. After these, a fifth door hides the sacred fire of transmutation. If all these tests are successfully passed, one achieves regeneration and rebirth. Then one enters the astral plane of emotions to resolve conflicts created by Light and Darkness.

The fourth volume, the *Book of the Sacred Cow*, contains the Legend of the Destruction of Humanity and introduces the means to destroy the cosmic snakes that obstruct the path of Ra, the sun. This is accomplished through ritual protection and by hindering the transfer of magical power. The notorious influence of the personal will — the selfishness of the personality — is herein described with the careful and extensive process by which it is worked upon through conscious death.

Volume five, called the *Book of the Hidden Chamber,* or the *Amduat,* describes the phase where one crosses the world of darkness. This work consists of initiations and the application of pure magic. It also contains initiatory keys: twelve chapters for each of the twelve hours of the night along with twelve of the sacred names. Volumes four and five teach the use of power that unlocks the passageway into cosmic existence. In *Inner Alchemy*, this stage is one of pure silence; the newly deceased commune with their Inner Presence and open up the particular gate corresponding to their individual development and energies.

The sixth and seventh volumes parallel one another. The former concerns the day, the latter the night. Together, they describe the rebirth of the sun and chart the day and night skies. For *Inner Alchemy*, these works correspond to the last two stages of the dying process, where the newly departed is guided in their next incarnation. By delineating real limits and learning new potential routes, the incarnating soul can embody a life of greater possibilities.

The last volume, the *Book of the Earth*, or *Book of Aker*, aligns with the phase of the Earth that promises a new consciousness. Both the past and future are included here. Aker, represented by two lion heads welcoming the sun, symbolises the union of opposites forged in the gold of transmutation — a preeminent alchemical symbol. Divided into four parts, Aker speaks of the birth of a star: the alchemical transformation of the human being into a member of the stellar cosmic kingdom.

THE TIBETAN TRADITION

According to the Tibetan tradition, upon death, the 'First Consciousness' evokes the initial state of greatest ascent. From that point on, the process trickles down through the different dimensions of Being, searching for the elements that resonate most with the newly departed and eventually resting at the most familiar and least resistant level. At this lower voltage and altitude, the 'Second Consciousness', that of the 'I AM', emerges. This marks the end of the first phase of the Spirit's journey. Up to this point, the human consciousness transits through higher dimensions without much awareness of them.

—

By delineating real limits and learning new potential routes, the incarnating soul can embody a life of greater possibilities.

—

The Tibetans

Now begins the second phase: the 'Reality of the Mind'. This period can feel like it lasts for days, though the exact timeframe differs for everyone. Throughout, the memory of life is replayed in a series of images and sensations. For those who have already awakened to their nature as Consciousness, these episodes will not prove difficult. Different kinds of awareness, each one representing a different element, confront the Spirit. Lights, symbols, images, and sounds all arise to illustrate and elicit a lifetime's worth of actions, powers, tendencies, aversions, and desires.

This second phase can be subdivided into two further stages. First, the soul desires to fuse with the energies or lights while the instincts of the personality resist the urge. Then the deceased relinquishes this internal struggle and passively accepts what is perceived. Beings, figures, or memories are often evoked at this point, many of a religious nature, to assist in the confrontation.

Between the second and third phases, the subject may be taken to centres of learning by guides or teachers, either for training or to rest after a traumatic life.

The recitation practices of the Tibetans also differ from those of the Egyptians. Within the latter culture, the ceremonies for their dead lasted a whole year and occurred on specific holidays. By contrast, the recitation of the Tibetan *Bardo Thodol* (known in the West as the *Tibetan Book of the Dead*) lasted forty-nine days. During this period, loved ones guide the deceased individual through the various 'realities' that confront them. Because the deceased's subtle senses are absorbed by intense apparitions, loved ones found it necessary to provide a conductive thread using sounds and sensations in a monotonous, repetitive, and constant rhythm. During the first few days, the recitation is done directly into the ear of the deceased; later, it is performed at home or in a familiar place.

THE AZTECS

The Aztec tradition resembles the shamanic rituals of warrior cultures such as the Inca, Japanese, and Vikings. They believed in heaven and hell, but the fate of the deceased depended not on how one lived but on how bravely one died. Specifically, those who either died in battle, were victims of sacrifice, or passed away during childbirth could reliably expect entrance into the House of the Sun in the East. As such, their bodies were burned so that the Spirit could freely climb this particular passage to heaven. After four years, it was believed they would return to Earth in the form of a hummingbird.

Others, however, were buried in the earth, since it was considered closer to hell. For the Aztecs, this underground world of the north was a place of deserts and fierce winds and was ruled by the god Mictlantecuhtli, who wore a skull mask and a layer of human bones. To get there, the soul had to travel through eight hellish layers, each more difficult than the last. After four years of horrific trials and torments, the dead would then be directed to the ninth hell — a place where their essence was burned and purified so that they could finally achieve eternal peace.

Aztec poets compared human life to a flower that sprouts from the earth, grows to the sky, blooms, and returns to the earth again. To prepare for their journey, the deceased were dressed in their best clothes and would carry a coin or piece of jade to pay for their trek. Those who could

—
Aztec poets compared human life to a flower that sprouts from the earth, grows to the sky, blooms, and returns to the earth again.
—

The Aztecs

afford it were accompanied by a yellow or red dog that would serve as a guardian. The rites they performed for the dead were similar to the Egyptians, including the construction of dedicated pyramids that were often larger and more majestic than their African counterparts.

This is all that is known of the former empire of the Americas, since the conquerors burned archives, temples, and other codices that chronicled their civilisation.

THE MAYA TRADITION

The Mayan tradition reminds us of very ancient civilisations, such as the Sumerians, the mythical Vedas, and even the Aborigines. They speak to us of other worlds, even other universes, and throughout this vast panorama, the eternal struggle between good and evil is perpetually fought. Their

The Mayans

prevailing legend of Quetzalcoatl, the Morning Star, whispers to us down through the centuries, reminding us of the archangelic works that weave the worlds together. While Quetzalcoatl and Mictlantecuhtli represent opposite poles of reality, the world is fundamentally united. Like Horus and Seth in Egyptian mythology, both sides unite to depict a greater underlying whole.

From a higher perspective, both archetypes — good and evil — are part of the evolutionary course that enhances the human-divine faculties of discernment and integrity. Similarly, in our own ordinary world, goodness is only fully grasped in the face of evil. Without night, we could never appreciate the light of day. To truly understand this higher reality, we must awaken and discover Osiris and Quetzalcoatl and, in doing so, unveil the realm of Heart Intelligence, which has always been there, waiting for our discovery.

EPILOGUE

Recognition must be given to the founders, teachers, tutors, and all those who have assisted in helping to make the Zulma Reyo School of Consciousness a reality. Each of them has contributed their unique selves to bring it into existence, and I am eternally indebted to them all. In addition, this book has been partly their creation, too, as together we have committed to the path of Inner Alchemy towards Consciousness, enabling me to refine and expand the knowledge.

To that end, I have included this testimony from one of our students, who states succinctly, and from the heart, the lessons to be learned when you do the hard work of ego-death. At times, you may want to give up, and when that moment occurs, I recommend that you reflect on these thoughts to encourage you.

This is what I have learned through the Zulma Reyo School of Consciousness:

- Not to focus on me but to go beyond myself, with a compassionate look at Humanity.
- To see my victim-self in its duality, in the inflated and deflated side of a square. Because the square may be balanced, but the circle represents Oneness.
- That reaction is tension, but a response is compassion, the compassion that emerges from mastery over myself.
- The simplicity of stepping aside with the magic of a single word: 'Stop!'
- That to be in a body is to feel fully present, and yet you are truly present only when you feel yourself feeling.
- That I am the manifestation of something bigger.
- I have no real need if I connect with that which I truly Am. This is how the doors of abundance open for me and everyone.
- That if I shed light onto my shadows, those same shadows will also dissolve in the collective astral. This is a great responsibility for myself and for the world.

- That I come from Light into the density of matter for the purpose of service and to raise the frequency of life itself: holding the Light.
- That any pending account is a monster which must be faced in the afterlife.
- That breathing creates space for new information because beliefs, thoughts, and emotions occupy space; however, the Divine Presence occupies it all.
- That my resistances are mere fears of looking at myself in total fullness.
- That I may be comfortable in my world of illusion, but when a small ray of Consciousness comes near, it reveals a new direction, and there is no turning back.
- To let go and see uncertainty as part of life, but if I fall into despair, I can always counter with the embrace and shelter of my Divine Presence.
- That greatness is in me because my Divine Presence is within.

ABOUT THE AUTHOR

Zulma Reyo is a spiritual teacher, visionary, and author whose transformative work bridges ancient wisdom and modern thought. Born in Puerto Rico, her multicultural upbringing instilled a profound sensitivity to both the seen and unseen dimensions of existence. From an early age, Zulma's deep communion with life's many layers inspired her to explore humanity's vast potential and develop a unique approach to connecting the worlds of form and spirit.

Educated in humanities, comparative literature, and romance languages at New York University, Zulma embarked on an eclectic journey of study that spanned pedagogy, primal therapy, psychotherapies, healing practices, and spiritual traditions. These diverse influences converged into Inner Alchemy, Zulma's pioneering system of energetic transformation that elevates vibrational frequencies to transmute or transform lower forms of expression.

As the founder of the Zulma Reyo School of Consciousness (ZRSOC), Zulma has created a transformative program that delves into the subtle dynamics of energy perception and spiritual leadership. This approach integrates meditation and pragmatism, training individuals in non-linear perception and reasoning. ZRSOC's distinctive methodology empowers students to translate insights from the illogical, inner realms into practical applications in the physical world. At its core, ZRSOC empowers clarity of vision, the responsible use of personal power, and the clearing of personal veils to access the Greater Self – the Soul. Students are guided to explore essential human questions: *What are my real priorities? What is really happening behind the surface? What is authenticity? How can I discern the true voice of my Soul from my personal longings?* By attuning to a frequency of true power, ZRSOC inspires its cohorts to foster profound and lasting change within themselves and the world.

Zulma's published works, including *Inner Alchemy* and *Emergence of Consciousness*, encapsulate her lifetime of study, offering transformative guidance to empower individuals to access their greater potential while fostering a profound connection to truth and service. www.zrsoc.com